ML
410
•H4
B83
1972

Bobillier, Marie,
1858-1918.

Haydn

DATE		

HAYDN

HAYDN

By
Michel Brenet
(Marie Bobillier) 1858 - 1918.

Translated by
C. LEONARD LEESE
With a commentary by
Sir W. H. HADOW

BOOKS FOR LIBRARIES PRESS

FREEPORT, NEW YORK

First Published 1919
Reprinted 1972

Library of Congress Cataloging in Publication Data

Bobillier, Marie, 1858-1918.
   Haydn.

   ([BCL/select bibliographies reprint series])
   Reprint of the 1919 ed.
   Bibliography: p.
   1. Haydn, Joseph, 1732-1809.
ML410.H4B83   1972   780'.924 [B]   79-39688
ISBN 0-8369-9930-4

PRINTED IN THE UNITED STATES OF AMERICA
BY
NEW WORLD BOOK MANUFACTURING CO., INC.
HALLANDALE, FLORIDA 33009

PREFACE

SO far as I am aware, this is the best available biography of Joseph Haydn. It does not come into comparison with Pohl's work, which was planned on a larger scale, and so far as it goes may take rank with Spitta's *Bach*, Jahn's *Mozart*, and Thayer's *Beethoven*: Pohl's work was left unfinished at his death and carries the narrative no further than 1790. Of the treatises and pamphlets catalogued in ' M. Brenet's ' bibliography some are abridgements, most are monographs on some particular aspect of Haydn's music; none is sufficient to occupy the vacant place. During the last forty years we have hoped that the material left by Pohl would be incorporated and completed in a final volume; this hope is not yet realized, and meanwhile the monument has been raised by other hands.

This volume appears, in its English dress, at an appropriate time. The neglect of Haydn, which ' M. Brenet ' deplores in her opening page, is passing away at any rate from this country: we are renewing, year by year, our enjoyment of his melody, his humour, and his translucent style. And as much of his noblest writing belongs to his old age, and is therefore outside the purview of Pohl's two volumes, we are specially ready to welcome a critical study which may not only focus our attention but aid and direct our judgement. For this office ' M. Brenet ' was well qualified. Her work was evidently a labour of love: she brought to it wide reading, tempered opinion, acute and critical insight, and a hand already trained in historical research: throughout the book there is abundant evidence that she possessed the two first requisites of a biographer, original talent and a genuine and discriminating sympathy.

It is natural that in so wide an area there should be topics which the reader could have wished to see further developed, and even statements which he may be inclined to call in question. We should like, for example,

b

to know on what ground it is said (p. 5) that Haydn's education at St. Stephen's 'fixed in his mind the principles of the instrumental quartet'. This is against the customary belief that he made his first acquaintance with these principles during the years of struggle which followed his departure from the school—the years in which he first came across the Sonatas of C. P. E. Bach and adapted their structural methods to the forces of concerted music. Again, though ' M. Brenet ' avoids the inveterate error which places Haydn's first symphony four years later than his first quartet (an error far more serious than any question of dates) she would have done service to the reader if she had enlarged (p. 109) on the simultaneous emergence of both forms from Haydn's ' Divertimenti ', and on the remarkable fact that both are represented in the six compositions which have been published as Op. 1. There is some reason for holding that Haydn wrote them for a small band of strings and wind; at any rate, Op. 1, No. 5, was omitted by him from his subsequent catalogue of string quartets and was published by Breitkopf with wind parts included. There is also some room for discussion on the difficult questions of the baryton and the lira (pp. 26-7 and 45). The former seems to have been used chiefly in its upper register—at least the few specimens of its music preserved at Eisenstadt contain only one note which could not be reached by the violin: the latter is not equivalent to the archiviola (which was one of its species as the theorbo was a species of lute) and it is probable that the instrument for which Haydn wrote was the ' lira da braccio '; since in one of the duets Haydn has cancelled the names of ' lira 1 and 2 ' and replaced them by those of flute and oboe. A more noticeable statement (p. 79) is that Haydn left an ' enormous number of motets ', many of them written at the instigation of his wife who wanted to turn them to account. On this the last word must lie with the definitive edition: Pohl's catalogue in

Grove contains only four motets, and even if we extend
the term to comprise offertories and other smaller
choral .compositions, together with excerpts from
oratorios (like *Insanae et vanae curae*) the number is not
large. Very possibly 'M. Brenet' is including spurious
works, which are clearly of no biographical relevance.

These, however, are matters of detail which have
very little bearing on the value of the book as a whole.
But there are three larger subjects on which, with all
respect and admiration, I would venture to join issue.
First, I think that not nearly enough has been said on
the relation of Haydn to his contemporaries, and particularly to Mozart and Beethoven. To say that
Haydn's visits to Vienna ' enabled him to meet his
rivals and receive the homage of his admirers' seems
to me in false proportion. His friendship with Mozart
was perhaps the noblest, certainly the most fruitful,
in all artistic history: not only did it remain unbroken
and unclouded from their first meeting till the time of
Mozart's death, but it exercised a deep influence upon
the compositions of both. ' It was Haydn ' said Mozart ' who first taught me to write a string quartet'.
' I declare before God ' said Haydn to Leopold Mozart
' that your son is the greatest composer of whom I have
ever heard ': and it is impossible to study their instrumental compositions from 1780 onwards without seeing
how much they were mutually indebted. Haydn's later
quartets, in particular, show traces of Mozart on which
it would have been well to lay more emphasis. The
account of Beethoven is not less perfunctory. It begins
with the hesitating statement (p. 52) that when Haydn
was feasted at Bonn in 1792 ' he may have noticed
Beethoven, who was to rejoin him and ask for lessons a
few months later '. Never before, I think, has any
doubt been thrown on the well-attested story that
Beethoven was formally presented to Haydn, showed
him a cantata, and was immediately and cordially accepted by him as a pupil. And the rest of the story,

which covers a period of some fourteen years, is dismissed in one rather disdainful sentence. The intercourse of the two greatest living composers deserved a rather more detailed narration.

The second point is one with which I feel some difficulty in dealing, since on it I have to reply to a very courteous challenge. ' M. Brenet ' is evidently unconvinced as to Haydn's employment of Croat folk-tunes, and since I am cited as a witness there is nothing for it but to offer myself for cross-examination. The story, so far as concerns myself, is as follows.

In 1894 or 1895 I discovered in the Taylorian Library at Oxford a copy of Dr. Kuhač's ' South Slavonic folk songs '. I knew no word of Croatian, and was therefore at that time restricted to the melodic evidence: but it needed no expert knowledge to see that some of the melodies were identical with themes of Haydn and that others bore a close resemblance to his style. That summer I went to Budapest for the Exhibition, and there, in a show-case, noticed Dr. Kuhač's pamphlet on ' Joseph Haydn and the South Slavonic Folk Songs '. On my return to Oxford I procured this and had it translated. The material seemed to me of such importance that I decided to make such use of it as could be allowed: and in the next summer vacation I went out to Agram to ask permission of Dr. Kuhač. Full permission was readily and generously accorded, and a little volume of mine, published in 1897, was the result. It may be added that on the way to Agram I visited Vienna, Rohrau, Eisenstadt, and Esterhaz; surveying the whole Haydn country, which had evidently been a colony of Southern Slavs, and spending as much time as I could in Prince Esterhazy's libraries.

So much for the witness: now for the testimony. And I would begin by demurring to a request which has all the appearance of reasonableness without any of the reality—that I should produce a collection of

Croat folk-songs, containing these melodies and of earlier date than Haydn. No doubt this would settle the question; it would throw a great deal of light on the battle of Arbela if we had a contemporary account in the Mesopotamian *Daily Courier*. But, unfortunately, these things are impossible. During the whole of Haydn's lifetime, not to speak of the generation before, there was no such thing as a printing press in Croatia: no literature, no editor of folk-songs, no settled alphabet. All these date from Gaj and Strossmayer in the nineteenth century: to expect them earlier is to show a want of historical imagination. The whole discussion must be on matters of internal evidence and probability: there is no other guide.

Secondly, it is not correct to say that the resemblances are confined to a few fragments, that they are confined to Lower Austria, or that they are confined to Haydn's later compositions. All these statements are wrong. Dr. Kuhač's pamphlet is before me as I write. It does not pretend to be exhaustive, but it quotes over thirty identities, most of which are not fragments but whole eight-bar or sixteen-bar melodies: they come from a great part of what is now Jugo-Slavia: the earliest of them is in a Cassation of 1765, others date from 1771 and 1774, and they come down to the Salomon Symphonies of 1794. In other words they extend across the forty most prolific years of Haydn's life.

It is hardly worth while ruling out the hypothesis of coincidence; and we are therefore left with two alternatives: one that the melodies were composed by the Croat peasants and adopted by Haydn, one that they were composed by Haydn and adopted by the Croat peasants. Let us bring the question to a crucial instance. The Service 'Hier liegt vor Deiner Majestät' was written by Haydn as an audacious jest at the expense of Prince Esterhazy: a *pièce d'occasion* intended for a single performance. It is a sequence of seven hymns, to German words, the tunes of all of which are

virtually or literally identical with known Slavonic folk-
songs. Which is the more likely—that these were
orally transmitted, like all early folk-songs, and that
Haydn found them and used them, or that the peasants
' heard them through the windows ', memorized them
at a single hearing, fitted them to secular words, and
carried them through the taverns and merry-makings
of their native villages ? The evidence in other cases is
equally strong; in some it is stronger. Three of the
melodies, for example, appear in the 7th Salomon
Symphony, which was written for London after the
Esterhazy Kapelle had been disbanded. Where and
how could the villagers have come across them ?

I believe that the disinclination to adopt what seems
to me the obvious view springs from a fear lest it
should be somewhat derogatory to Haydn—that it
should involve him in some charge of plagiarism. No
charge could be more unjust. Haydn was brought up
from childhood in the midst of folk-songs; he heard
them sung night after night at his father's house, he
heard them in Vienna during his boyhood, he heard
them at the Engel in Eisenstadt which he used to
frequent after his day's official work was over. They
were bone of his bone and flesh of his flesh: what more
natural that he should make the same use of them as
Burns of the Scottish songs or Shakespeare of the
Warwickshire proverbs ? No one calls Bach plagiarist for
using the Lutheran Chorales, or Moussorgsky for using
the songs of Russia, or Stanford the songs of Ireland.

The last point of discussion is one on which ' M.
Brenet ' speaks with the authority of long study, but
has reached conclusions which my own reading does
not happen to corroborate. On page 103 it is said that
the Suite, in the hands of seventeenth-century composers consisted of ' an overture followed by several
dances ', and that at some unspecified time—the
earliest date given is 1748—the overture was detached
and appeared ' as an independent work in three move-

ments '. Both these statements seem to me inaccurate.
The earliest Suites were combinations of Pavan and
Galliard: then other dance forms were added or substituted until by the beginning of the eighteenth century there was a fairly established scheme of Allemande,
Courante, Sarabande, and Gigue, with which various
forms—prelude, gavotte, bourrée, etc.—might optionally be associated. But the prelude (it is usually called
prelude, not overture) was never an essential part of the
Suite; it does not find any place, for example, in Bach's
French Suites, and in its earliest form, it is far too
slender to bear the weight that ' M. Brenet ' lays upon
it.* The orchestral overture, as a separate piece in three
movements, was developed not from it but from the
exigencies of opera and oratorio; both in its French and
in its Italian form it comes to the concert hall from the
theatre, not from the chamber: its primitive nucleus is
the Toccata of Monteverde's *Orfeo*, and the two types
were established by Lulli about the middle of the
seventeenth century and by Scarlatti some twenty
years before its close. There are, indeed, some signs of
haste in the part of the volume devoted to chamber
music, as, for instance, that the first eighteen quartets
contain five movements apiece, that Haydn wrote no
quartets between 1771 and 1781 (the set published as
Op. 20 belongs to 1774), and more noticeably that in
the famous Op. 33 the change from minuet to scherzo
is ' merely verbal '. These quartets were called Gli
Scherzi, because, as their composer himself said, their
lyric movements were ' in a new style '. That of Op.
33, No. 5, for example, shows a good deal more than
a verbal difference from a minuet.

I have enlarged on these points because the book is
so thoughtful and so well-written that it affords
abundant material for debate. And it is quite possible

* Two of the Partitas in the first volume of Bach: *Clavierübung*
contain introductions which follow the form of the French Overture.
But they are more than half a century too late to serve as evidence.

that I look at music too much from one point of view
and care too exclusively for certain aspects with which
other students are less concerned. It is only fair to add
that I have found the whole volume pleasant and
profitable and that I have learned a great deal from it.
On one matter it has specially earned my gratitude by
correcting an obvious mistake of my own. In giving
the number of Haydn's symphonies as ' about 153 ' I
no doubt included the overtures (for which indeed I
have Haydn's warrant), but I also included several
manuscripts, the authenticity of which has since been
denied. I did it for the same reason which inspired
Dr. Johnson's definition of ' pastern ' and I am glad
to have the opportunity of acknowledging my error.
The number 104, which is given in the present catalogue, should no doubt be substituted.

It is part of ' M. Brenet's ' skill in presentation that
she has introduced us in this volume not only to a
great genius but to a most agreeable companion. ' Anyone who looks at me' said Haydn ' can see that I am
a good sort of fellow '; there is probably no artist to
whom we can more justly apply Pope's line—

> In wit a man, simplicity a child.

And his music is all irradiated with the same geniality
and kindliness as his character: it can be humorous but
never cruel, adventurous but never ugly, it can feel
deeply without being sentimental and talk learnedly
without being pedantic. Indeed, one of his most con-
spicuous gifts is the lightness and ease with which he
carries his technique: like Mozart, he so assimilated it
in early life that he could play with it and make it into
a holiday tale. It is a matter of great satisfaction that
this cheerful pleasant music is once more coming to
its own—' bringing a breeze of health from wholesome
places ', and setting us at our ease by its own frank
confidence of a welcome.

1925   W. H. HADOW.

INTRODUCTION

WHEN Joseph Haydn was presented to King George III of England, the latter said to him by way of compliment 'You have composed a great deal, Dr. Haydn'. He replied, with the modesty that was natural to him, ' Yes, sire, rather more than was wise '. In the course of a long and always industrious life, he had, indeed, written so much that he no longer remembered many of his works. Some of his manuscripts had been lost. He knew that the duties of office and the importunity of admirers had wrung from him many a hasty page, and in the end he came to attribute real importance to a part only of his work, that part upon which his success and fame undoubtedly rested.

As his followers continued in the path where he had been a pioneer, they and the public gradually allowed him to drop out of sight; and thus, with the passing of each decade, his work figured less and less prominently in the general memory. In theory, the place which he occupies in the line of great musicians, between Bach and Beethoven, is not contested. But in practice, owing to the comparatively rare performance of his works, knowledge of them has been confined within the narrow limits which convention lays down as a necessary minimum for acquaintance with a poet or an artist. With an air of disdain, our contemporaries are pleased to rank Haydn among the classics of youth, and imagine that, in order to like him, one must be in one's first or second childhood. Beginners have a frank affection for him. They look upon him as a cheerful grandparent who can tell pretty stories. When they reach the age at which man seeks in a work of art the reflection of his troubled soul, they turn away from a happy, peaceful, equable master, who has never felt the uncertainty of fate or the storms of passion. Those alone can listen to him attentively and find pleasure in his message whom the flight of time has taught to take a wider view and to judge from a higher and more tolerant standpoint.

Partly for this indirect reason, popular taste is not responsive to Haydn's music. Moreover, the enormous number of his works has made it difficult to collect and classify, and even to identify, them all. Thus it has come about that, while complete editions have been published or are in preparation of the works of almost all the great masters of the past, from Palestrina, Lassus, and Vittoria to Purcell, Schütz, Handel, Bach, Mozart, Rameau, and Grétry, and on to Beethoven, Schubert, and Berlioz, there was no similar undertaking for those of Haydn, until in 1909 the approaching celebration of the centenary of his death led at last to the launching of a scheme which it was estimated would take at least fifteen years to complete, and would require eighty volumes or sixteen thousand pages.

To postpone any new study of Haydn until all the difficulties had been smoothed away by the execution of this vast plan would have been a mistaken view of the part which is assigned to historical criticism in our own day. Our object is not to rehabilitate a composer whose work is recognized by all, nor to revise the judgement of the past upon his work, but simply to recall to the distracted ear of the younger generation, lured by other heroes towards wider horizons, the already distant but ever captivating echo of the music of Haydn.

HIS LIFE

I

HAYDN'S early days were passed in a poor, one-storied cottage with a thatched roof in Rohrau, a village of Lower Austria neither beautiful nor important, close to the banks of the Leitha, which forms the Hungarian frontier. His father, Matthias Haydn, was a wagon-maker by trade; his mother, Maria Anna Koller, had been cook to some of the neighbouring gentry. Franz Josef, born during the night of 31st March-1st April 1732, and baptized the following day in the Catholic church of Rohrau, was the second of twelve children, half of whom died in infancy. The others who survived were two brothers, Johann Michael, born on 14th September 1737 and Johann Evangelist, some years younger, both of whom also became musicians, and three sisters, Franziska, the eldest, Anna Maria, who married a blacksmith named Philipp Fröhlich, and Anna Katerina, who became the wife of a certain Näher, a musketeer. Their mother died on 23rd February 1744 at the age of 44. Their father remarried and had five children by his second wife, none of whom lived. He died at the age of sixty-five on 12th September 1763.

This village craftsman was a great lover of song. Although he could not read music, he sang in a tenor voice, accompanying himself by ear on a harp. On Sundays, his cottage resounded with airs of dance, song, and psalm, which he was never tired of singing over and again with his wife, children, and neighbours. One day, when a fiddler came to join in the concert, little Josef made for himself, with two pieces of wood picked up in the workshop, a make-believe instrument, on which the company were astonished to see him imitate all the gestures of the stranger. A schoolmaster cousin thought this amusement was a sign of musical

3

ability, which he wished to develop. Sepperl, as the child was called familiarly, was put in his charge, and went with him to Hainburg.

According to the custom of the time, this first master of Haydn, Johann Matthias Frankh, united the office of teacher in a country school with that of choirmaster of a Catholic church. His lessons—seed scattered in an extraordinarily fertile soil—soon enabled the little peasant boy to sing his part in a mass, to play little pieces on the harpsichord and the violin, and—a feat which attracted attention—to take the kettledrums without preparation in a procession.

In spite of his talent, Haydn's life would probably have been spent obscurely in a post similar to that of his cousin Frankh, had Providence not brought to Hainburg a person of some importance, Johann Georg Reutter the younger, composer to the Imperial Court and *Kapellmeister* of the cathedral of St. Stephen at Vienna. While travelling in search of boy-recruits for the choir of this church, he made a halt with the parish priest of Hainburg, who, in conjunction with Frankh, was anxious to show off the musical resources of his parish. Whether Reutter himself singled out the ' weak but agreeable ' voice of Haydn, or whether the school-master specially pointed out his young kinsman, the fact remains that, after a short test, he engaged him.

' Sepperl's ' entrance into St. Stephen's was, how-ever, delayed for a year. He was in his eighth year when he set out for Vienna.

A cathedral school in those days in the Austrian capital only differed in its repertory from similar in-stitutions in France. There, as in France, a small num-ber of boys, four, six, at most eight, chosen for their voices, lived together in the care of a master, and re-ceived in exchange for their frequent presence in the choir, lessons in the catechism, Latin, and singing. Either as pupils or as masters, nearly all the composers of former days passed through the Protestant or

Catholic cathedral-schools, which were the forcing-houses in which their genius appeared and developed.

According to one of his commentators, the great Bach, author of the Church Cantatas, for the most part owed his skill in the combination of voices to his experience as a choirboy*; and Haydn's sojourn in the cathedral at Vienna not only gave him skill with voices but also accustomed him to polyphonic writing, and fixed in his mind for all time the essential principles of melodic development and of the construction of the instrumental quartet.

The time spent by the young musician at St.Stephen's was valuable mainly from the practical point of view, through his daily participation in the services; for Reutter, the nominal *Kapellmeister* who had engaged him, paid as little attention to him as to the rest of his pupils.

He was a busy man, much in the public eye after the Emperor ennobled him in 1740. Born at Vienna in 1707, pupil of his father, to whose post he succeeded, he wrote without intermission operas, dramatic cantatas, serenades, masses, oratorios, and motets, as required by his triple office of Composer to the Court, *Kapellmeister* of St. Stephen's, and later of the Imperial Chapel. After the death of Fux, Reutter was the prototype of the official musician in the Austrian Empire. His biographer, Stollbrock, has successfully defended him against the reproach of neglecting Haydn's education†; he had many other things to do besides teaching rudiments, plain-song, and technique to children, and custom authorized him to delegate his duties to a few experienced members of the choir. His mistake was in failing to discern Haydn's exceptional ability, and in treating him on the same footing as the other little

* W. Rüst, quoted by A. Pirro, *l'Esthétique de J. S. Bach*, p. 402.

† Stollbrock, *Leben und Wirken des kk. Hofkapellmeisters J. G. Reutter junior*, in *Vierteljahrsschrift für Musikwissenschaft*, 8th year, 1892, p. 198.

choirboys. Here, too, there are excuses, for in all
cathedral choirs there were many gifted children, who
had to be made capable singers as quickly as possible
and who did not always display any further talent before their departure.

Thus, Haydn's two masters who taught him to sing,
and to play a little on the harpsichord and violin, were
Adam Gegenbauer, a member of the choir who was
also a violinist and copyist, and a tenor, Ignaz Finster-
busch, a man of fashion and a collector of pictures,
Turkish weapons, and silver-buttoned coats. Their
lessons were perfunctory, to such an extent that Haydn,
in his old age, used to say that he had no real masters
but had taught himself entirely by listening and reading
and by observing everything. The desire to write music
which had early taken possession of him had received
neither guidance nor encouragement. The instruction
at St. Stephen's included no course in theory, and when,
one day, Reutter came across the manuscript of a *Salve
Regina* which the child, with the youthful audacity of
a schoolboy writing tragedy in rhyme, had just composed *for twelve voices*, he only laughed at it and told
the ' foolish lad ' to go back to the elements of his art.

Haydn was thus compelled to learn from the example
of the cathedral repertory. This repertory, as varied as
it was extensive, consisted of the works of Reutter and
his father, the first Georg Reutter (1656-1738), the
strictly classical works of Johann Joseph Fux (1660-
1741), and the copious products of composers of
Italian origin or culture who had lived in Vienna or
were still in official positions there: Caldara (1670-
1736), the most prolific of all, Matteo Palotta of
Palermo (1689-1758), and Giuseppe Bonno (1710-
1788), a recent arrival from Naples, where an Imperial
grant had facilitated his studies. The masses, Te
Deums, and motets of these indefatigable musicians
accumulated by dozens upon the stalls of the choir.
Some of these were still written *a capella* ; the majority

required an orchestral accompaniment. Scarcely one survived; scarcely one crossed the Austrian frontier. Recent publications have rescued from oblivion the great scholastic talent of Fux alone, whose *Missa canonica* was a marvel of composition. If little Sepperl ever sang his part in this, it must have been a revelation to him of the austere beauty with which contrapuntal theory can clothe itself.

The municipality of Vienna provided with such extreme economy for the food and upkeep of the choir-boys of St. Stephen's, that it was found advisable to allow them, from time to time, to go and earn else-where a more substantial meal, or a few shillings. Either as singers, they took part in musical entertain-ments, or as kitchen hands, they joined the ranks of the attendants at banquets. In the first case, the pro-gramme consisted of serenades or secular cantatas, and in the second, custom dictated that every fashionable dinner should be accompanied by music. Thus the children became acquainted with the various types of secular composition. Perhaps it was while running with an armful of plates from the kitchen to the dining-room, in the mansion of some great nobleman that Haydn first heard an orchestra playing minuets, over-tures, and symphonies.

A proof of his usefulness in the choir of St. Stephen's may be found in the fact that his young brother Johann Michael was allowed to join him there in 1745. He had a voice of wide range, and was so studious that, after a few months' residence, he was able to act as deputy for the organist. The two Haydns spent nearly three years together in the cathedral choir. Then came Haydn's change of voice, which made it necessary for him to leave. From all the stories which have been handed down about this event—of cutting the tails of wigs, and other mischievous tricks, of threatened punishments from which the young man escaped by a sudden departure—we gather only an impression of his lively, playful, and humorous nature. These are the characteristics which he retained until his old age, and they throw light on many of his melodies.

Whatever may have been the manner of his exit from St. Stephen's, the fact remains that, at the age of seventeen, in the month of November 1749, he was thrown upon the streets of Vienna almost as ill-provided in talent as in cash; for without voice, of what use was his skill in singing? He had not learned to play any instrument well enough to enable him to find employment. His musical vocation was, however, sure, his temper brave, and his habits frugal enough for him to accept cheerfully the companionship of poverty, to which, indeed, he had been accustomed from childhood.

Fate, which at Hainburg had thrown Reutter in his path, was destined to provide many another lucky meeting for him. The first was with a parish singer, Spangler, whom Haydn came across by chance one morning after a night in the open air. This colleague was himself only a poor devil. Married and a father, he had, however, a home into which he received the ex-choirboy; and the latter, sure of sleeping under cover, if not of dining every day, began to look about him at the life of the great city.

At that time, there was no city in any German-speaking country so pleasant, so cheerful, and so musical as Vienna. Fifty years later, Reichardt could describe it as the second musical capital, Paris holding the first place. He based his judgement on the presence of celebrated composers and virtuosi, and on the number and importance of the public institutions—theatres, concert-halls, and choirs which he had noticed in France. Had he studied the matter more closely, the German traveller would have discovered that of the two cities, Vienna was the one in which music had more devotees and was a more intimate part of the national life. In 1749, Haydn found there, even in the humblest ranks, an atmosphere saturated with music in which his career was to unfold, rising, so to speak, from the unknown depths to the brilliant surface of the artistic ocean.

No circumstances could have been more in harmony with his natural gifts. Born of the people, and belonging to them heart and soul, he flourished, after leaving St. Stephen's, like a young plant brought back from a hot-house to its native soil. The echoes which reached him of the music of the time were no more than fragments heard through half-opened windows—the odours of a feast to which he was not invited, and which would not have greatly pleased him. For the aristocratic circles of Vienna lived for little but the brilliant and superficial works of the Neapolitan school, and moreover, dilettantism raged in the acute form of amateur compositions. How can a king or a nobleman better display his favourable disposition to music than by cultivating the art himself? The Emperor, Charles VI, who died in the same year that Haydn was admitted to St. Stephen's, had followed the example of Ferdinand III, Leopold I, and Joseph I, and had composed *Miserere* with orchestra.* His daughter, Maria Theresa, did not go to such lengths in the education of the archdukes and archduchesses, but she took care that they should acquire some technical skill, through the lessons of Wagenseil, Joseph Steffan, and Wenzel Pürck. The depleted finances of the empire benefited in this way, for performances were very economical when all the various parts could be distributed among members of the reigning family and their circle.

The Viennese public who only heard the Italian opera in the Schlosstheater (theatre of the royal palace) on the days of free admission, such as the birthdays of the Emperor and Empress, found at the Kärnthnerthor Theater performances in German, which

* The *Musikalische Werke der Kaiser Ferdinand III, Leopold I, und Joseph I* were published in 1892 by Artaria, at Vienna, in two volumes, through the industry of Guido Adler.

mingled comedy, music, and farce. And at carnival time, on improvised stages, there were entertainments by clowns and marionettes.

Since 1750, there had been in the concert room at the palace private concerts, imitated from the meetings of the *Concert Spirituel* in Paris, which was famed through all Europe. To these were soon added performances of a similar nature in Zur Mehlgrube, and soon other more modest concerts sprang up and multiplied, in hostelries, in gardens, and in the streets. From that time forward, the Austrian capital merited what modern travellers have said of it—that ' nowhere are there happier people or people who show more inventiveness in their amusements', and that ' at the hour when work ceases, houses, streets, and parks become one immense scene of dancing and merriment'. In Haydn's time, serenades especially had become so much an established custom that few evenings during the summer months passed without the sound of instrumental or choral music in the open streets, in compliment to the inmates of some house. Sometimes the performances were at the expense of a wealthy citizen wishing to pay a compliment or to honour a festivity, or sometimes they were given on the direct initiative of the musicians, who were always certain of receiving the meagre reward they expected in victuals, drink, or money.

To join these little bands of serenaders and to stroll with them, violin in hand, through the streets of the town, was almost a sufficient means of livelihood. Haydn lived, like the grasshoppers, in this way all the summer, and in winter found occupation in taverns and places of amusement by his playing and by composing minuets.

In the garret where Spangler gave him refuge, he was not free from anxieties. To go on indefinitely with this fiddler's life was not to be contemplated. To return to Rohrau, where his parents were struggling to bring

up their numerous family, seemed a still more unsatis-
factory solution. His mother wished him to join a
religious order, and although he felt little vocation for
it, he thought of joining the Servites, an order founded
in Florence about 1232 in honour of the Virgin Mary,
of which the monasteries still existed in the eighteenth
century in Austria and in Italy. According to his
biographers, what he appreciated most in this calling
was the certainty of having something to eat every day.
Probably he also considered the possibility of continuing his musical studies in the cloisters. Not only
might he become organist or choirmaster in a monastery, but there were abundant examples of monks who
had won wide and lasting fame as composers and
theorists*.

In a burst of piety, natural to a mind occupied by
such thoughts, Haydn decided, in the spring of 1750,
to join the pilgrims going to the sanctuary of Mariazell
in Styria†.

Presenting himself boldly to the monk in charge of
the choir, he offered to show him various vocal compositions which he had written, and which he was
anxious to be allowed to interpret himself in the chapel.
The priest, however, importuned too often for personal favours, soon packed him off with the remark
that there were too many vagabonds coming from
Vienna and pretending to be musicians, who did not
know the A B C of their trade. Determined to realize
his ambition at all costs, Haydn resorted to stratagem.
At the hour of the service, he slipped into the group
of singers, begged one of them to let him take his part
for a few moments, and added his voice to the choir so

* The most famous was Padre Martini, at that time the oracle of
Europe in matters of musical theory. Haydn may also have heard ex-
tolled the works and teaching of Father Czernohorsky, for many years
Kapellmeister at Prag.

† On this pilgrimage a small volume has been published: *Maria-
Zell in Steiermark: Entwurf einer Monographie des berühmten Wall-
fahrtsortes*, by H. Rogl, Vienna, 1903.

unexpectedly and so surely that the prior noticed it
and wished to meet the musician. As a reward he was
allowed to live for a week at the table of the monks,
and to make a collection which enabled him to return
in good spirits to Vienna.

Better days were in store for him. Spangler, who
had changed his abode, could no longer give him hos-
pitality. But just at that moment he obtained from a
friend, a lace merchant, the loan of a hundred and fifty
florins, immediate and free of interest. Installed in his
own apartment, with an old worm-eaten harpsichord
and a few books of music, he quickly became ' the
happiest of men ' and translated his gladness into
musical compositions.

As a good Christian, he began with a mass. Then
he wrote some pieces for the open-air orchestras, and,
in the winter of 1751-2, a short dramatic work for
which he had obtained a commission, thanks to one
of the serenades in which he continued to take part.
One evening, when he had played some pieces of his
own composition in the street with his companions,
one of his hearers who had been listening at a window
came down to make inquiries about the author. Before
the performers separated, he took him into his house,
set him before the harpsichord, dictated to him a subject for an improvisation, and gave him the manuscript
of a comedy and a pantomime with instructions to
compose music for them.

This man of rapid enthusiasm and decision was a
popular actor-author, Joseph Kurz. His comedy,
entitled *Der Neue Krumme Teufel*, was in the satirical
manner and the performances were quickly suspended.
Thus Haydn had little time to enjoy his first success
in the theatre, and for a long time had to abandon hope
of reappearing there.

In choosing for his home an attic in the old St.
Michael's House of the Barnabites, situated on the
Kohlmarkt, not far from the Graben, the young musician,

quite unconsciously, laid the foundations of his fortune; for in this building lived the poet Metastasio,
through whom he soon made the acquaintance of
Porpora.

Until then, Haydn had received no lessons to guide
him in the art of composition. He studied certain
treatises—the *Gradus ad Parnassum* of Fux* and the
books of Mattheson†—and such works of celebrated
musicians as his slender resources permitted him to
buy, notably the brand-new Sonatas of Carl Philipp
Emmanuel Bach‡. In proportion as his little knowledge increased, he made use of it in teaching the young.
The chance of proximity threw among his pupils a
little girl of ten, Marianne Martinez, whose parents
shared one floor of the house with their friend Metastasio. It was in this way that Haydn became familiar
with the sovereign poet, a court pensioner, and official
representative of musical tragedy, and in virtue thereof,
collaborator of all the masters of Italian opera.

Through Metastasio Haydn came to know Nicolo
Porpora§. Already old and weary, but with a dazzling
prestige, due quite as much to the success of his singing pupils as to his composition, the latter had just left
Dresden to settle in Vienna.

He was often called the ' patriarch of melody ', the
reference being both to his skill in the art of writing
for the voice and to his talent for the interpretation of
vocal music, of which he seemed to hold all the secrets.
The faults of his work arose out of the qualities of his
method. Aiming at virtuosity alone, it was bound to

* The original Latin edition of Fux's treatise was published in 1715,
and the German translation by Mizler in 1742.

† The principal treatises of Mattheson (1681-1764) were the *Kleine
General-Bass Schule* (1735), the *Grosse General-Bass Schule* (1731),
and *Der Vollkommene Capellmeister* (1739).

‡ Six sonatas of Emmanuel Bach, dedicated to the King of Prussia,
appeared in 1742; the six sonatas appended to the *Versuch über die
wahre Art das Clavier zu spielen* in 1753.

§ Porpora was born at Naples in 1685. He died there in 1767.

perish with its interpreters. It was through his renown
as a teacher that Porpora attracted Haydn, and in his
desire to acquire, under a famous master, ' the true
foundations of musical knowledge', of which his reading gave him only a superficial idea, he was ready to
submit to any conditions, reasonable or unreasonable.
Heroic legends tell in symbolic language of the trials
imposed on the bold adventurers who go in quest of
knowledge. There was not the smallest atom of romance
in Haydn's conduct. Instead of crossing enchanted
forests and vanquishing dragons, he became, for several
months, Porpora's valet, brushed his shabby clothes
and put his wig in order, meanwhile waiting for a
favourable moment when he might receive advice or
show one of his manuscripts.* The old Neapolitan was
morose, boorish, dirty, and miserly. At the least provo-
cation, he broke into angry words, interspersing the
vocabulary of the gutter with the names of all the
animals in a farmyard. Yet, in the midst of these in-
vectives, the silent disciple received the explanation
desired. The most profitable moments were those in
which Porpora made use of him to accompany his singing pupils on the harpsichord, and it was in order to
retain his services for this purpose that the terrible
professor took him to Mannersdorf, a watering-place
to which he followed the Venetian ambassador.

Haydn's meeting at about this time, with an Austrian
nobleman, Karl Joseph von Fürnberg, was of great
importance to his career. This personage, who shared
the general taste of the Viennese aristocracy for chamber
music, engaged the young musician as violinist and
took him to his residence at Weinzierl, near Vienna,
where every day he played instrumental music with
amateurs or paid musicians. For the musical evenings
at Weinzierl Haydn composed eighteen string quartets.

* George Sand, in her interminable novel, *Consuelo*, has considerably embroidered the theme of Haydn's youth and his relations with
Porpora.

Thus it was through Fürnberg, as he recalled in his old age to Griesinger, that he made his first experiments in a form of composition in which he attained his greatest success.

On Fürnberg's recommendation, about 1759, Haydn joined the household of Count Maximilian von Morzin, Chamberlain and Privy Councillor to the Emperor. He lived in Prag or Vienna in winter, and in summer at a newly-built castle on his estate at Lukavec, in Bohemia. With the title of ' composer and director of music ', and emoluments of 200 florins a year, with his lodging and food at the table of the upper servants, Haydn found himself at the head of a little party of twelve or fifteen musicians, for whom he wrote *divertissements* and little symphonies. This sojourn with von Morzin was the stepping-stone which enabled him to climb to a better post. Prince Paul Anton Esterhazy, when on a visit to Lukavec, had noticed the merit of the pieces played before him, and when von Morzin, in 1761, was suddenly obliged to cut down his expenses, and dismissed his musicians, Prince Esterhazy at once took Haydn into his service. This, the chief event of the master's career, coincides with the most important happening in his private life—his marriage.

Affairs of the heart play a very small part in Haydn's life, and the historians have not been able to devote many pages to them, whether to adorn his biography with romantic passages, or to support the analysis of his works by a sentimental commentary. The story of his marriage throws a vivid light upon the mixture of simplicity, kindness, and tranquil endurance which formed the basis of his character, and which provides an explanation of the moral content of his work.

One of the humble families whom Haydn visited in Vienna was that of the wigmaker, Johann Peter Keller, whose two daughters took lessons from him on the harpsichord. Attracted by the younger, he resolved

to make her his wife without the knowledge of von
Morzin, who made it a rule to employ no married
servant. When he approached the father, he learned
that the fate of the girl was otherwise decided, and
that she was just on the point of taking the veil. Whether
from surprise, weakness, indifference, or, it is said,
gratitude for pecuniary help previously accepted,
Haydn became engaged, at the father's desire, to the
older instead of the younger daughter, and on 26th
November 1760, he married Anna Maria Keller, who
was three years older than he, and whose capricious,
sharp, and quarrelsome temper could not but be known
to him. Possibly because he hoped for improvement,
he was the more resigned. He retained all his equable
temperament and all his natural gaiety in this ill-assorted
union with this ' infernal creature ', who bore him no
children, and who gave no thought to him except to
annoy him, and none to his works except to cut up
the sheets of paper into curl-papers or pastry-cases.

The only romance in Haydn's life began twenty
years later. It is a prosaic story which may as well be
told at once without regard to chronological order,
for it had no effect on his musical development.

In the month of March 1779, an Italian couple
arrived at Prince Esterhazy's to help with the music.
The husband, Antonio Polzelli, was a violinist. The
wife, Luigia Polzelli, born Moreschi, a singer, was a
Neapolitan, nineteen years old, agreeable though not
beautiful, with a voice that was sweet but of small
compass, and whose mediocre talent only fitted her
for subordinate parts. Both of them were engaged for
two years, but were dismissed after eighteen months,
in December 1780, and returned to Italy, where the
young woman appeared on the stage in the smaller
towns.

A similarity in misfortunes created a bond of sympathy between Haydn and Mme. Polzelli, for just as
the composer suffered through the character of his

wife, so had the singer many grievances against her husband. Being a clever and a very provident person, she made no stumbling-block of Haydn's being twenty-eight years older than she, and soon the two lovers were in perfect agreement in the wish that a double accident might speedily free each of them from an intolerable partner and allow them to find in lawful marriage a solace for their past and present troubles. Antonio Polzelli, who first fulfilled their desires, died only after ten years. The interval was filled by a correspondence in which Luigia was never tired of asking for money, nor Haydn of sending it. The most that the excellent man permitted himself was to remark on one occasion that six hundred gulden in a year was a large figure for a man without fortune, who lived by his own labours.

When the good news reached him of the death of the violinist, all his confidence returned and he hastened to congratulate the widow.

'DEAR POLZELLI,—Perhaps that moment may yet arrive which we have so often desired, when two pairs of eyes will be closed. Here is one pair shut! But what of the other? May it be as God wills!'

The other pair of eyes, those of Haydn's wife, remained open until 20th March 1800. As Mme. Polzelli was then only forty, and Haydn was sixty-eight, she was in no hurry to press for marriage, and contented herself with a promise in the form of a private deed, which was worded thus: 'I, the undersigned, promise Signora Loisa Polzelli, that, in case I should think of marrying again, I will take no other wife than the said Loisa Polzelli; and if I remain a widower, I promise the said Polzelli to leave her after my decease an annual income for life of three hundred florins in Viennese money. In witness whereof, and in satisfaction of all legal requirements, I sign myself Joseph Haydn, Kapellmeister to His Highness Prince Esterhazy. Vienna, 23rd May 1800.'

Whereupon Mme. Polzelli, who had signed nothing, married a singer named Luigi Franchi*.

*
* *

Paul Anton Esterhazy of Galantha, whose service Haydn had entered after leaving Count von Morzin, belonged to one of the noblest families of Hungary and bore the title of Prince, conferred as an hereditary distinction by the Emperor Charles VI. His usual residence, some thirty miles from Vienna, was the castle of Eisenstadt†, an enormous square building, flanked by seven towers, and encircled by a moat, which was erected in 1683 near the western shore of the Neusiedler See, the remnant of an inland sea which at one time covered the Hungarian plains. Around it stretched a monotonous landscape, vast and green, as far as eye could reach, chequered by woods, moors, and enormous marshes, alternately dried up and inundated by the floods of the Danube and its tributaries, the Raabe and the Leitha. A sparse population, the *Heide-bauern*, eked out a meagre livelihood on these barren lands, where all the life was concentrated in the castle. There the Prince kept up a veritable court, with almost regal pomp. This nobleman was indeed a sovereign on a small scale. He was able, during the Seven Years' War, to place at the disposal of Maria Theresa a complete regiment of Hussars, raised, mounted, and

---

* She died in 1832. Mme. Polzelli had two sons, the younger of whom she entrusted to Haydn, so that he might take charge of his musical education, and more particularly, that he might pay for it. Inevitably, there was talk of a direct relationship between this young man and Haydn. These suspicions are belied by the master's two wills, the first of which mentions the young Polzelli only as the recipient of an insignificant legacy, while the second makes no provision for him at all. For the complete history of Haydn's relations with Mme. Polzelli, see C. F. Pohl, *Joseph Haydn*, vol. ii, pp. 92 ff., and for the text of the wills, Nohl, *Musiker-Briefe*, pp. 61 ff.

† The Magyar name of Eisenstadt is Kismarton.

trained at his own expense, and provided with a staff
of twenty-four officers. Paul Anton Esterhazy bore
the title of Field-marshal in the Imperial army, and had
for some time held the post of ambassador at Naples.
When he took Haydn as second *Kapellmeister* he was
a little more than fifty years old. His natural taste for
music had been fostered by the training and example
of his mother, Princess Maria Octavia, who was early
a widow and thus for long responsible for the education of her son and the management of his estates.
Under her administration the household musicians
had become so numerous as to necessitate the appointment of a *Kapellmeister*. The choice of the Princess had
fallen upon Gregorius Joseph Werner, whose appointment dated from 10th May 1728, and who was still
in office when Haydn joined him in 1761.

C. F. Pohl has published* the text of the agreement
signed at Vienna on 1st May 1761 by Prince Esterhazy
represented by a secretary, and Joseph Haydn, de-
fining in fourteen clauses the conditions of appointment
of the new assistant *Kapellmeister*. This is a remarkable
document, which throws light not only upon the life
of Haydn, but upon the history of music in Germany
throughout the eighteenth century. One who is not
familiar, among other things, with the humiliations
endured by Mozart at the hands of the Bishop of Salzburg would find proof in this document of the servile
position even of the leading musicians employed in
an aristocratic household. Musical duties and material
details of service are here enumerated in a curious order,
which would seem to give these latter the chief importance.

Werner's advanced age† is first of all invoked to
explain the necessity for appointing an assistant, in
the person of Joseph Haydn, who is to be under his
orders. His Highness expresses the hope that Haydn

* C. F. Pohl, *Joseph Haydn*, Vol. I, pp. 391 ff.
† He was sixty-six.

will conduct himself circumspectly as befits an officer of the household (*Hausoffizier*) in a princely residence, that he will be sober, quiet, honest, not ' brutal ' with his inferiors, but polite and of modest demeanour. His first duty, when music is performed in presence of His Highness, is to see that all his subordinates wear their uniform. Not only must he, Joseph Haydn, be neat in his attire, but he must take care that all those under him shall be equally so, that they shall appear with clean linen and white stockings, with their wigs powdered and worn either in a net or with a pigtail, so long as all do the same. The assistant shall behave towards the musicians in such an exemplary manner that the latter may model themselves upon him. He will avoid all familiarity with them, particularly in eating and drinking, so as not to diminish the respect due to him from his subordinates, and so as to avoid incidents out of which disputes and misunderstandings might arise. By order of His Highness, the assistant *Kapellmeister* will compose all the necessary music. He will divulge his new compositions to no one, still less will he allow copies to be taken of them, but he will reserve them solely for the service of His Highness. And he will write nothing for anyone else without having asked and obtained His Highness's gracious permission. Every day, whether His Highness is in residence at Vienna or on his estates, Joseph Haydn will wait in the ante-chamber before and after dinner, to find out whether there will be music, and to take orders. Immediately on receiving them, he will pass them on to the other musicians. He will see that the latter are assembled at the appointed time, and will keep a register of absence and unpunctuality. If, in spite of all precautions, dissensions, quarrels, or disputes should arise among the musicians, the assistant *Kapellmeister* must attend to them and deal with them according to the circumstances in such manner that His Highness may not be bothered with foolish troubles.

However, if anything serious should arise which Joseph Haydn cannot set right himself, he will respectfully report it to His Highness. He will take charge of all the music and the instruments so that nothing may be destroyed or damaged through negligence, for which he will be held responsible. It will be his business to teach the singers, so that they may not forget in the country what they learned from famous masters in Vienna at great trouble and expense; and if he plays several instruments, he must keep himself in practice upon all of them.

On reaching the tenth clause, the drafter of the agreement declares it useless to set down on paper all the other obligations attaching to the office of assistant *Kapellmeister*, but states that His Highness hopes that Joseph Haydn will fulfil all his duties and will obey with the greatest exactitude all the orders he may receive from His Highness, and that he will use all his zeal and his skill to place the music on a footing which will do him honour and render him worthy of His Highness's favour. His salary will be 400 Rhenish florins a year, payable quarterly. During the time that is spent on the country estates, the assistant *Kapellmeister* will either eat with the domestic staff or receive half a gulden a day for his food.

The agreement was to cover a period of at least three years. Should Haydn wish to seek his fortune elsewhere at the end of this time, he promised to make known his intention six months in advance. His Highness, on his part, not only stated his intention of keeping Haydn in his service during that length of time, but expressed the intention to reserve for him the full directorship, provided he was entirely satisfied with his ability. Otherwise, he reserved the right to dismiss him at any time.

The livery which Haydn wore, according to the description of a function held at Eisenstadt, was of dark red cloth, braided with gold. But during the many

years that Haydn spent with the Esterhazys, the family
changed their colours, for in a portrait which repre-
sents Haydn at the age of sixty, the uniform consists
of a pale blue coat with silver embroidery and buttons,
opening over a vest of the same, with white collar and
cuffs. Between the net and the pigtail, of which the
choice was offered him, Haydn preferred the pigtail,
and remained faithful to it to the end of his life, in spite
of all changes of fashion.

The amount of music that was played daily in an
aristocratic household was really formidable. The
musicians used to play whenever required for the
pleasure of their lord or to add an amenity to the daily
life, before, during, and after meals, in the evening at
concerts or for dancing, and on Sundays at Mass.
Dittersdorf, in his Memoirs, speaks of an Austrian
count whose orchestra was continually employed every
day from five o'clock to eleven, playing in succession
four symphonies by one composer, and then several
by another. In a second case, twelve concertos by
Benda were played straight off the reel; and at the
Bishop of Grosswardein's, Dittersdorf, in one evening,
conducted or performed one long and one short cantata, two long symphonies and one short one, and a
violin concerto, all of his own composition*.

In the castle of Eisenstadt, the musical performances, except those during meals, took place, sometimes in a large hall equipped as a theatre, and
sometimes in an elegant but smaller drawing-room.
The tiny chapel could not accommodate an orchestra,
and therefore, upon solemn occasions, the whole household attended the village church.

The musical staff under Werner's direction consisted of about fifteen persons. During the first year of
Haydn's engagement, this number was increased to
twenty-one: five violins, one violoncello, one double-
bass, one flute, two oboes, two bassoons, two horns,

* *Dittersdorf's Lebensbeschreibung*, pp. 50, 141.

one organist, two sopranos, one contralto, two tenors, and one bass. The first violin was named Luigi Tomasini; the 'cellist was Joseph Weigl, father of the future composer of comic operas; Carl Friberth was considered a good tenor, and the horn-players, who had a high reputation, were named Steinmüller and Franz. This organization was destined to receive a vigorous impetus by the accession of a new prince.

Haydn had not completed his first year at Eisenstadt when Paul Anton Esterhazy died on 18th March 1762. As he had no children by his marriage with the Marchesa di Lunati-Visconti, the heir to the title and the entailed estates was his brother Nicolas, born on 18th December 1714, and married in 1737 to a daughter of Count Ferdinand von Weissenwolf. With him the new customs of the Hungarian nobility were to take definite form. In close relationship with the Viennese court ever since the famous scenes in the Hungarian Diet and the coronation of Maria Theresa at Pressburg, the nobles had become sedulous guests at the Imperial Palace at Vienna and at the castles of Schönbrunn and Laxenburg. They had renounced both the speech and the costume of their ancestors; they talked French and German, travelled in France, and readily allowed themselves to be Germanized or Europeanized. Nicolas Esterhazy had visited Paris and Versailles. When he came into possession of the family estates, he resolved to build a palace comparable to that of the King of France, chose for its site a hunting-box near the southern end of the Neusiedler See, and displayed in its construction an extravagance which won for him the title of ' Magnificent '. The buildings of the new residence, which the Prince called by his own name, Esterhaz, were ready for occupation in 1766. Nicolas removed his establishment and settled there permanently, rarely leaving the place himself except for short winter visits to Vienna. Built in the Italian style, with a profusion of balconies,

colonnades, and statues, the castle of Esterhaz astonished
all visitors by its magnificence. Besides the state rooms,
it contained one hundred and twenty-six chambers,
variously decorated, and rooms full of curios, pictures,
Chinese treasures, and books. A separate building
contained the opera house, which was large enough
to hold four hundred spectators. Another building
was set apart for the marionettes. The park, which
lacked none of the essential features—maze, classical
temples, grottoes, Chinese pagodas, artificial waterfalls
—was of great extent and offered to guests at the castle
the pleasures of riding, hunting, and fishing.

In this luxurious setting, thirty years of Haydn's
life were to pass by with uneventful regularity. In
virtue of his agreement, his person and his talent formed
an integral part of the outward luxury of the place.
The *Kapellmeister* was one of the wheels of the machine
which existed solely to minister to the entertainment
of the prince and to uphold the fame of his establishment. In all the noblemen's dwellings, large and small,
of Germany, Austria, Hungary, and Bohemia, hundreds
of musicians at that time led similar lives. Like Haydn,
they rose with the dawn to write, in the silent morning
hours, new compositions which they rehearsed during
the day and conducted in the evening. It was scarcely
possible for them to trouble about the ultimate fate of
the works which accumulated in the music cupboards,
dictated as they usually were either by circumstances
or by the caprice of the person they served. Still less
did they think of breaking the bars of their cage. Until
Beethoven, who refused to wear the yoke, the great
majority of German musicians held it an enviable
honour to belong to a master, and were content with a
slavery which freed them from the material cares of
life. At Esterhaz the vocalists and the instrumentalists were lodged, with the rest of the domestic staff,
in the servants' quarters, where the *Kapellmeister* was
allowed a suite of three rooms, married men were

given two rooms, and bachelors shared one room between two.

Prince Nicolas took a personal interest in the music. In imitation of several sovereigns of his time, he willingly took part in the chamber concerts, and posed as a virtuoso and connoisseur. His formal entry into Eisenstadt in 1762 was celebrated by musical and dramatic festivals which Haydn organized and took part in. Towards the end of the same year, the marriage of Prince Nicolas's eldest son, Count Anton, with the Countess Maria Theresa Erdödy offered the musician a brilliant opportunity for his first essay in composition for the theatre. Between the *Te Deum* sung in the chapel and the music played during the wedding feast, a performance was given of an Italian pastoral by Haydn, *Acide e Galatea*.

Two years later, for the Prince's return from the coronation, at Frankfurt-am-Main, of the Archduke. Joseph as King of the Romans, Haydn composed a cantata and a *Te Deum*. But it seems that Nicolas Esterhazy, more exacting or more ambitious under the recollections of his recent travels, was not satisfied with these works or with their performance, for, in 1765, a curt and severe note was addressed to Haydn to recall him to his duties. In this document, he was instructed to have ready in triplicate within a week a detailed inventory of the music and instruments; to keep in the cupboards provided for the purpose all the musical scores required for performances; to see to the repair of the instruments; to take proper care that the choristers discharged their duties during services in a seemly and efficient manner; to assemble all the musicians, twice a week, from two to four o'clock, when the prince was away, in the appointed chamber, and to give two concerts, with the object of preventing anyone from absenting himself without leave; to send to the prince every fortnight a detailed report containing the names of those who had misbehaved themselves in any way; and, finally, ' to display more assiduity than heretofore in composition, especially of pieces for the viol da gamba ', for which instrument he had hitherto written little, and to send a ' neat and clean ' copy of each to the prince.

This last order related to the favourite amusement of the prince, who played the baryton* and was very proud of his skill. There is a story of one of his musicians, the 'cellist, Adam Kraft, who, thinking to flatter him, learnt to play the baryton himself, and composed some trios for two barytons and bass, in which he played second to the prince. One day, when he was tactless enough in a passage where the two instruments answered each other to give himself a solo, Nicolas interrupted the performance, demanded the score, tried to play it, and, defeated by some difficulty, handed it back to Kraft with orders that, in future, he was to ' write no solos except for my own part, because to wish to play better than I would merit blame, not praise '. By a like excess of zeal, Haydn committed a similar blunder. At the time, probably, when he was ordered to compose more for the baryton, he practised the instrument in secret—a step which might have seemed necessary for a thorough understanding of its possibilities and its technique—, but when his new accomplishment was disclosed, he was given to understand that he had something better to do. He took it to heart and contented himself with providing plenty of ' neat and clean ' copies. He composed for the baryton, alone or accompanied, nearly two hundred pieces suited to the capacity of their recipient. Almost all were lost in the two fires, which, in 1768 and 1776, destroyed part of the Castle of Esterhaz. To preserve

* The baryton or *viola di bordone* (*viola bastarda*) was a viola da gamba furnished, like the viola d'amore, with catgut strings set in vibration by the bow and with others of metal, placed under the finger-board and vibrating sympathetically. A most interesting and complete description of this instrument and the music written for it can be found in the essay by L. Greilsamer in the monthly *S.I.M.*, 1910, no. 1.

some of these, not from destruction, but from oblivion, Haydn arranged them in different instrumental combinations, for the baryton was already uncommon, and was soon to disappear*.

On 3rd March 1766, a few months before the move from Eisenstadt to Esterhaz, ' old Werner ' had died. C. F. Pohl said of him that he had been ' buried alive ' with the Esterhazy family†, and, indeed his talent—to which Haydn paid homage by arranging and publishing six of his fugues for string quintet—was squandered in unnoticed labours. If the works of genius written by his successor enjoyed a happier fate, it was not entirely due to their merits. The increased musical luxury of Prince Nicolas Esterhazy's little court, the brilliance of his receptions, his desire that some of the fame won by the productions of his *Kapellmeister* should be reflected upon his house—all this effectively helped to establish and increase Haydn's reputation. As early as 1764, several of his instrumental compositions were printed in Paris; in 1766, the *Wiener Diarium* described him as ' our national idol ', boasted of the qualities of his works, and declared him to be the equal in music of Gellert in poetry—which must be considered high praise at the time when the vogue of the author of the *Fables* and the *Odes* was at its zenith.

The visits of distinguished foreigners to Esterhaz máy in some measure have created a public for Haydn's works and compensated for the isolation to which the duties of his post condemned him. In honour of guests of note, festivities were organized which kept the musicians occupied with little respite. Prince Louis de Rohan, French Ambassador at

* In 1789, one of Prince Esterhazy's musicians, Carl Franz, visited Paris and gave two recitals at the Palais-Royal, at which he played the baryton, an instrument unknown to French audiences. Probably his repertory consisted mainly of works by Haydn.

† C. F. Pohl, *Joseph Haydn*, Vol. I, p. 209.

Vienna*, was there in 1772, and declared Esterhaz a second Versailles. The Empress Maria Theresa passed three days at the castle in 1773 and heard Haydn's opera for marionettes, *L'Infedelta Delusa,* and the symphony which still bears her name. The following year the Archduke Ferdinand was a guest. Later, when the Grand Duke Paul of Russia, travelling incognito under the name of Count to the North, was expected, Haydn wrote the opera *Orlando Paladino* for his entertainment; but as this project was abandoned, it was given in the presence of Prince Esterhazy and his circle alone.

Probably because nearly all musicians still wore livery, the custom of conferring orders and decorations upon them had not yet been established†. It was by the gift of snuff-boxes set with precious stones or filled with pieces of gold that the Grand Duke Paul of Russia conveyed to Haydn the pleasure he experienced at Vienna on hearing some of his quartets, and that the King of Spain rewarded him for sending him a number of scores. Prince von Öttingen-Wallerstein, for whom he had composed symphonies, made him a similar present. A diamond ring came from the King of Prussia in return for a dedication. Count Erdödy, who had sent him Pleyel as a pupil, paid for the lessons with the gift of a carriage and pair, which Prince Esterhazy was good enough to maintain in his stables. Such presents, rendered honourable by custom, represented the *Kapellmeister's* share in the gratuities distributed to servants in the castle by visitors to Esterhaz.

Haydn's salary, originally fixed at four hundred florins, was raised by successive increments to seven

* Louis René Edouard, Prince de Rohan, later Cardinal-Bishop of Strassburg, who became notorious through the affair of the diamond necklace.

† The title of *Knight of the Golden Spur,* conferred on Gluck and Mozart by the Pope, was an honour as exceptional as the patent of nobility and the Order of St. Michael granted by the King of France to Rameau and Royer.

hundred and eighty-two florins, to which must be added bonuses for exceptional services or particularly successful works. 'I have received three pieces from Haydn' writes Prince Nicolas from Vienna to his steward 'which please me exceedingly. You will pay him twelve ducats from my cash-box, and tell him to do me six more pieces in the same style and two solos.'

Besides the works of Haydn, the Italian company resident at the castle drew its repertory from operas performed at the Imperial Theatre at Vienna, the authors of which were Piccinni, Sacchini, Sarti, Anfossi, Paisiello, Traetta, and Cimarosa. Prince Nicolas's tastes inclined towards the *dramma giocoso*, which was more suited to the scale and style of his own opera house than the *opera seria*. His infatuation for marionettes lasted only a few years, during which time Haydn was obliged to write several little pieces especially suitable to this form of entertainment. He had also to compose overtures, entr'actes, and incidental music for comedies But he had to redouble his activities for the concerts of chamber music for which his co-operation was in daily request, and for the special private concerts at which he produced four or five new symphonies each year.

As relaxation from his labours, Haydn liked to take long walks in the neighbourhood of the castle. A fall from his horse while at Count von Morzin's had turned him against riding for the rest of his life. Fishing and hunting, for which the Neusiedler See and the surrounding forests offered abundant opportunities, were his favourite amusements. He was vain of his skill in shooting, and showed as much pride at having killed with one shot three hazel-hens which were served at the Empress's table, as in the subsequent performance before Her Majesty of some of his best works.

The orchestra he conducted was like a family to him, the younger members being at once pupils and subordinates, and calling him affectionately *papa*.

From time to time there appeared among them certain
artists whose fame spread beyond this little musical
kingdom: the violinists Antonio Rosetti (1745-1792)
and Nicolas Mestrino (1748-1790), the 'cellist Anton
Kraft (1752-1820), and the harpist Johann Baptist
Krumpholtz (died 1790). The veterans of the company, Friberth, Tomasini, and Weigl, became his
friends. The last-named, who married the singer Anna
Maria Scheffstoss, chose Haydn as godfather, and
later as master, to his son Joseph Weigl (1766-1846),
who was destined to win the favour of the German
public during the first quarter of the nineteenth century by his comic opera *Die Schweizerische Familie.*

In addition to the personnel placed under Haydn's
orders, there came to Esterhaz from time to time young
people seeking his advice or desiring a course of lessons.
Among these were Georg Distler of Vienna (died 1798),
who became concert-master to the Duke of Württem-
berg; Niemecz, a Franciscan friar, who resided at
Esterhaz as librarian, and whose instrumental music
had some success; and especially Ignaz Pleyel (1757-
1831), whom Count Erdödy sent to him in 1776, and
who was the most brilliant of his pupils. 'Some quartets
have just appeared' wrote Mozart to his father in 1784
' by a certain Pleyel, a pupil of Joseph Haydn. If you
do not know them, try to get them. It is worth the
trouble. They are very well written and very charming. You will recognize his master at once. It will be a
fortunate thing for music if Pleyel, in due time, is able
to fill Haydn's place.'*

For a short time, it seemed that Mozart's wish would
be fulfilled. Pleyel, who was gifted with extreme
melodic facility, succeeded in assimilating his master's
methods to such a degree that he was able to deceive
the musical public upon the value of his work and
sometimes upon the actual authorship. His quartets,
all his chamber music, and his pianoforte sonatas,

* *Lettres de Mozart*, French translation by H. de Curzon, p. 531.

enjoyed a popularity hitherto without parallel, but which disappeared for ever when the lapse of time had given the public an opportunity to reflect upon its judgements. The man whose success had equalled that of Haydn and Mozart, and whose works were distributed in various editions and arrangements, in numbers which were prodigious at that time, is represented to-day in classical collections or selections, by two or three pieces preserved as historical curiosities*.

Antonio Rosetti, who was Pleyel's fellow-pupil, seems to have equalled him in merit and nearly so in productivity, without attaining the same degree of popularity. He, too, won his greatest success by following in Haydn's footsteps in instrumental music. Nearly the same thing may be said of Paul Wranitzky (1756-1808), who was conductor of an orchestra in Vienna, and who composed a few ballets in addition to symphonies and concertos. Beethoven, Lessel, Neukomm, and Seyfried became Haydn's pupils later, after his journeys to London. The long list which C. F. Pohl† has compiled would be still longer if the names were added of those whose desire to attract the public attention tempted them to adopt the title of ' pupil of Haydn ' in virtue of some slight occasional instruction they may have received. Among these were Johann Baptist Kolb and Georg Anton Walter, whose quartets and trios bear the coveted distinction on the title-page.

Of Haydn's work as teacher there remains in the archives of the castle of Eisenstadt a copy of a manuscript, dated from Esterhaz, 22nd September 1789, which is a simple summary of the theory of counterpoint, taken from the works of Fux. But Beethoven's experience later and a few recorded remarks of Pleyel show clearly that Haydn's aptitude for teaching was slight, and that he conveyed instruction mainly by example.

* The *Répertoire encyclopédique du pianiste*, by H. Parent, includes only four pieces by Pleyel, Vol. I, p. 73.

† In Grove's *Dictionary of Music*, article *Haydn*.

Neither the laborious life he led with Prince Nicolas nor the affections of the musicians surrounding him tempted him to forget his kindred and his native village. Rohrau was not far from Eisenstadt, and the removal of the court to Esterhaz increased the distance only by the length of the lake. Many proofs, the last and most convincing being the master's two wills, attest his solicitude for his family. In 1765, he sent for his youngest brother, Johann Evangelist, a musician of moderate ability, and enrolled him as tenor in the chapel choir. He remained in the Prince's service until 1790, and continued to reside at Eisenstadt even after his retirement. He lived there until 1805 in close touch with his illustrious brother who watched attentively over his welfare.

Haydn's intercourse with his other brother, Johann Michael, on the contrary, became, by force of circumstances very infrequent. The reader will remember that Michael, who was born at Rohrau on 14th September 1737, joined Joseph in the choir of St. Stephen's, where they spent several years together. Then fate separated them, and Michael went to Temesvar, in Hungary, and then to Grosswardein (Nagy-Varda) to the Bishop Firmian, whom he left in 1762 to settle at Salzburg, as musical director to the Archbishop Sigismund Schrattenbach. To this post, which he retained under the succeeding prelate, Jerome Colloredo, Michael Haydn added, in 1777, the functions of organist in the Church of the Trinity. By his marriage, in 1768, with Maria Magdalena Lipp, a singer at the archiepiscopal court, he had an only child whose premature death for long darkened his life and his thoughts. In every way, as Michael himself observed with some jealousy, he was less lucky than his brother, though nearly as talented. Perhaps it was ' out of spite ', as popular opinion has it, or to console himself for the injustices of fate, that he gave way little by little to a too great fondness for the bottle. His meetings with

Joseph remained cordial but were only occasional. In 1798, they met in Vienna; a little later at Eisenstadt. Johann died at Salzburg on 10th August 1806, like Johann Evangelist before his elder brother. Mozart, who had lived near him, but never liked him, made much of his works. Several of his motets, choruses, and symphonies entitle him to lasting fame.

* *
*

Esterhaz, after all, was for Haydn only a gilded cage. Once Prince Nicolas was installed in the splendid palace which he had built, and which he was continually occupied in improving, his winter visits to Vienna were cut down to very short periods. When his whole household did not follow him, his musicians, tied by their engagements, and ' belonging ' to him, according to the ideas of the time, had great difficulty in obtaining regular leave. Many a time the tale has been told of Haydn's ' Farewell ' symphony, which he composed about 1773, by way of petition to convey to the Prince the ' sighs and complaints ' of the members of the orchestra, detained that year even later than usual, far from Vienna and their own families. The new symphony was announced as the last item in a concert at which the Prince was present. Its unusual key, F sharp minor, suggested in itself a hidden meaning, which was not disclosed in the first allegro, but was announced by the timid sweetness of the adagio with its muted violins, and which the finale made clear as though by a sudden resolve. After about a hundred bars, all the instruments stopped suddenly, on the dominant of the key; when a return to the principal key was expected, a fragment of the adagio reappeared interwoven with a new theme, soon divided into four parts for violins. In another moment, the second horn and the first oboe blew out the candles of their music-stands and quietly left the hall. The bassoon, silent until then, seemed to try to replace them, and twice, in unison

D

with the second violin, began the first notes of the
original motif; but, immediately abandoning his part,
he disappeared in his turn. Gradually all the lights
were extinguished, all the musicians stole away, until
the Prince's favorite, Tomasini, the first violin, and a
second violin, were left alone at their posts in the semi-
darkness. Very sadly, with muted instruments, their
last accents seemed to fade away in the night, and
Haydn, alone at his desk was preparing, not without
anxiety, to go out too, when Nicolas Esterhazy called
him and announced that he had understood the musicians' request and that they might leave the next day*.

Haydn's placid endurance, which sustained him
through all the difficult circumstances of his life, and
the optimism which helped him to see the bright side
of things led him to say with all sincerity to the friends
of his old age: ' My prince was always satisfied with
my work. Not only had I the encouragement of his
constant approval, but being at the head of an orchestra entirely under my orders, I was able to make experiments and try effects. Cut off from the rest of the
world, I had nothing to worry about, and I was compelled to be original.'† Sometimes, however, this
isolation became burdensome, and his regrets are
shown in his intimate corrrespondence. Though he
did not share Mozart's opinion‡ on the necessity of

---

* There are many versions of this anecdote. We follow that of C. F.
Pohl, *Joseph Haydn*, Vol. II, p. 56. This symphony was very successful in Germany and in London and Paris, where it was given with
the same setting as at Esterhaz. Pleyel and Dittersdorf thought the
effect so happy that they copied it. It is affirmed that Haydn wrote
a sequel to it, *The Return*, but the latter symphony is lost.

† See the conversations of Haydn, reported by Dies and Griesinger.

‡ ' I assure you ' wrote Mozart to his father on 11th September
1778 ' that if people do not travel (those at least who are concerned
with art and science), they are indeed poor creatures. . . . A man of
second-rate ability remains always second-rate, whether he travels or
not, but a man of *superior* talent (and I cannot deny myself this without
injustice) would go wrong if he stayed always in the same place. . . .'
Lettres de Mozart, French translation by H. de Curzon, p. 251.

travel for artistic development, he would have liked
sometimes to broaden his horizon, and particularly to
visit Italy, whose magic name had echoed in his ears
from his youth onwards as the country of the *bel canto*
and of the most brilliant musical culture. This dream was
never realized, and the whole time that he lived with
Prince Nicolas Esterhazy, Haydn had to content himself with two or three months each year in the Austrian
capital as his sole means of contact with European
musicians. At most, he might be able to make the
acquaintance of his rivals and enjoy the homage of his
admirers. There also, the greater part of his time was
taken up by his ordinary duties; for when Prince
Nicolas took his musicians outside Esterhaz, he made
a point of displaying their talent. In March 1770, they
had to give a performance, at Baron Sommeran's in
Vienna, of an opera by Haydn *Lo Speziale*, already
produced at Esterhaz. In 1772, he took his *Kapellmeister* to Pressburg to stay with Count Anton Grassal-
kowicz, to conduct this nobleman's orchestra during
a festival in honour of the Archduke Albrecht. In 1777
all Prince Esterhazy's musicians went to the Imperial
Palace at Schönbrunn, to give an opera by Haydn
and a piece for marionettes. The composer must have
been greatly honoured at having to conduct the music
during his Sovereign's dinner.

The entertainments given in Vienna during the
winter of 1781-2 in honour of the Grand Duke Paul
of Russia, in which all the Austro-Hungarian aristocracy took part, brought together Haydn and Mozart.
It is not known exactly at what date the two masters became acquainted. About 1774 Mozart was studying
the works of Haydn, and the latter, on his side, was
to be greatly influenced by those of his young rival,
though only much later, at the end of his career and
after Mozart's death. During the winter of 1784 they
had new opportunities of meeting at Vienna. From
Mozart's letters, we learn that he played on no less

than nine occasions at Prince Esterhazy's musical evenings. The following year, Mozart dedicated to Haydn, in terms which prove a real friendship, tinged with a respect due to their great difference in age, a set of six quartets which they had probably played together. There is a contemporary record of an informal meeting at the house of the composer Storace, in Vienna, where Haydn, Mozart, Dittersdorf, and Vanhal played together in the same quartet. On a similar occasion Haydn took the second violin and Mozart the viola. Ditters von Dittersdorf (1739-1799), an excellent violinist and composer of the day, and a man of great good humour, had been in the service of the Prince of Saxe-Hildburghausen and the Bishop of Grosswardein before entering the Bishop of Breslau's establishment, where he combined his musical post with the stewardship of forests*. Wanhal (1739-1813) held no official post and lived in comparative poverty in Vienna on his earnings as a teacher and a 'cellist, and on the profits from his instrumental compositions, which were considered equal at the time to those of Haydn.

About the same period, there were to be seen also in the Austrian capital Paisiello (1741-1816) returning from St. Petersburg, and Giuseppe Sarti (1729-1802), who was on his way there as musical director to Catherine II; the violinist Jarnovic (Giovanni Giornovicchi, 1745-1804); and the 'cellist Johann Baptist Mara (1744-1808) with his wife, the celebrated singer Gertrud Mara, born Schmeling (1750-1833). More than ever, Vienna was becoming the Mecca of musicians, who gathered there from all parts of the world. It was very natural that Haydn should try to profit by his visits there to have his works performed. He actually succeeded in getting one or two of his operas staged

* This office, which was reserved by custom for the nobility, brought him in 1773 the imperial authority to take noble rank, and to change his plebeian name of Ditters to Ditters von Dittersdorf.

in the smaller theatres; but in 1776, *La Vera Costanza*, which he had composed expressly for the Court theatre, was rejected as a result of mean intrigues. The crowd of mediocrities who held most of the official sinecures had everything to fear from the triumph of such men of genius as Haydn and Mozart, and jealously guarded the approaches to the imperial palace.

The opposition, as regards Haydn, dated from the time when Florian Gassmann (1729-1774) was *Kapell-meister* to Maria Theresa. Joseph Bonno (1710-1788), who succeeded him, was equally unfriendly, and under Joseph II, the violinist Franz Kreibich made use of his personal favour with the sovereign to prevent the performance of Haydn's quartets in the Court con-certs. A strange dispute which arose between Haydn and the Society of Musicians (*Tonkünstler-Societät*) shows that the same influences were ranged against him in other quarters. This society was founded at Vienna in 1771 to collect and distribute benevolent funds and pensions for the widows and orphans of musicians. A few years later Haydn expressed a desire to join, and in 1775, at one of the concerts given annually for the benefit of these funds, he arranged a performance by the soloists of Prince Esterhazy of an oratorio of his, *Il Ritorno di Tobia*, the rights in which he handed over to the Society. By paying the ordinary subscription, Haydn thought to provide for his wife in case of widowhood. But the committee, presided over by Joseph Bonno, tried to exact from him a capital payment of three hundred florins on the pretext that he did not live in Vienna, and moreover, claimed the right to his artistic services without payment. To which the offended composer replied that 'the liberal arts and, in particular, music, could not be held to commercial bondage', and he withdrew his candidature.

In 1781, however, the committee, thinking a second performance of *Il Ritorno di Tobia* would be profitable, asked the author to make some cuts and other alterations. Haydn replied that if the Society would promise him some free tickets or any other recompense for his trouble and expenses, he would do the work required, and would himself conduct the rehearsals and the performance, which would unquestionably increase the receipts by a round hundred ducats. The committee, instead of being grateful for this offer, objected to Haydn's claims, and declared that, because of the future consequences which such an arrangement might entail, they would choose another oratorio, *Elena*, by Hasse.

It was ten years before relations were resumed, during which the Society did very well out of performances of Haydn's symphonies at its concerts. It was only in 1797 that the committee, on the proposal of Paul Wranitzky, a former pupil of Haydn, offered him free membership, ' in the desire to atone for their former insolence towards him, and in recognition of the profits obtained from the performances of his works '*.

Outside artistic circles, Haydn found in Vienna warm admirers and devoted friends. In 1785, yielding to the fashion set by Joseph II, he joined, like Mozart, a masonic lodge, *Die wahre Eintracht* (True Concord), which served as a kind of club for artists and men of letters†. Among the Viennese middle classes, he had many precious friendships. The houses of the merchants Tost and Puschberg and of Doctor Genzinger were open to him. It was to the wife of this last, ' the noble, esteemed, and excellent Frau von Genzinger ', that he wrote his regrets when the happy winter season was over, and he had to accustom himself again to the monotonous life at Esterhaz. The sorrow with which his heart overflowed were not all for the loss of his

---

* Hanslick, *Geschichte des Concertwesens in Wien*, pp. 15 ff.

† C. F. Pohl, *Joseph Haydn*, Vol. I, p. 207. Mozart belonged to another Lodge, *Hope Achieved*.

musical pleasures. With these were mingled other and
more prosaic regrets which were fittingly confided
to a German housewife. ' Here I am again in solitude
—abandoned—like a poor orphan—almost without
human companionship—sad—filled with the memory
of happy days gone by,—yes, unfortunately, gone by.
And who knows when these pleasant days will return ? This happy company, a whole circle of friends
united in heart and soul, all those delightful musical
evenings, of which one can think, but which one cannot describe, where are all these joys? They are past,
and it will be long before they come again. Let your
ladyship not be surprised that I have been so long in
expressing my gratitude. I found everything upside-
down at home. For three days I have not known whether
I was musical director or musical lackey. I have been
inconsolable. All my rooms were in disorder. My
pianoforte, which formerly I loved so much, was capricious, disobedient, and irritated rather than calmed
me. I could scarcely sleep. I was tormented with
dreams. The best of them was when I thought I heard
the opera *Le Nozze di Figaro*. The wretched north
wind woke me and nearly tore my nightcap from my
head. In three days I lost twenty pounds in weight,
for the excellent Viennese food is far away. Ah yes, I
said to myself, while I was obliged to eat a slice of a
cow half a century old, instead of delicious beef, old
mutton with mushrooms instead of Ragou [*sic*] with
forcemeat balls, a roast tough as leather instead of
Bohemian pheasant, a coarse salad instead of sweet
and delicious oranges, dried-up apples and nuts instead of pastries, etc. . . . Ah yes, I thought, if I
only had now some of the delicacies I could not eat in
Vienna. Here, at Esterhaz, nobody asks me " Will
you have your chocolate with or without milk? " " Do
you prefer your coffee black or with cream? " " What
can I offer you, my dear Haydn? Will you have a
vanilla or a pineapple ice ? " If I only had a bit of

good Parmesan cheese, especially on fast days to help down the macaroni and spaghetti. . . .'*

To the publisher Artaria, Haydn wrote, not of food, but of business. It was from this point of view that he said briefly but sadly: ' It is my misfortune to live in the country. The greatest obstacle [to experiments in opera] is the length of time my prince stays in the country.'

Haydn's works were at first circulated in copies made by hand, and some few of them were issued by foreign publishers—in Paris 1764, and Amsterdam 1765—before they were printed in their native country. Artaria of Vienna began to publish them in 1769. But it was chiefly after 1780 that Haydn's relations with publishers became both frequent and fruitful, and that he not only had dealings with Artaria but was in touch with Forster, Longman, and Bland of London, Breitkopf of Leipzig, and Sieber and Naderman of Paris. He managed his business affairs very well. According to the custom of the time, he first made sure of a number of subscribers, soliciting them himself by letter, to whom he offered a ' correct copy ' of his unpublished works, in order of application at a price fixed in advance—six ducats, for example, in 1781, for a collection of quartets ' in an entirely new style'. Later he settled the conditions of publication of the same work in such a way that it could only be placed on sale and distributed to the general public after all the subscribers' copies had been issued: a complicated system which did not work very smoothly, particularly when, to add to other annoyances, a clever but grasping publisher, whom Haydn termed a usurer, was in too great a hurry to print or announce the work.

He had also to protect himself against pirates who

* Letter dated 9th February 1790. Haydn's letters to Frau von Genzinger were published by Karajan in his pamphlet, *Haydn in London*, pp. 57 ff., and reproduced by Nohl in his *Musiker-Briefe*, in which the letters to Artaria are also found.

made money by issuing unauthorized and often inaccurate editions, and whose cunning in obtaining
advance copies of successful pieces baffled all precautions. To avoid an injury which was not exclusively
material, since the beauty, the purity, and the authenticity of a work might suffer grievously, Mozart used
to shut up under lock and key the copyist he was obliged
to employ*; and Haydn, finding in the person of the
' faithful Elssler ' that incredible rarity, a perfectly
honest secretary, attached him to himself as copyist,
factotum, half-companion, and half-valet.

In his negotiations with publishers Haydn was well
able to point out the merits of his works and the chances
of success which, for instance, the title *Laudon* gave
to a symphony†. Nor did he fail to raise the amount of
his royalties as his fame increased. Thus, after only a
few years, he pushed up the amount exacted from
Artaria for twelve minuets for orchestra, from twelve
to twenty-four ducats. Again, in demanding twenty
guineas from Forster for a set of six pieces, he alleged
that he was offered five times as much elsewhere. His
zeal in producing new works, which sometimes led
him to lose sight of his older publications, and his
haste in replying to business offers caused him, on one
occasion, to take a very unfortunate step. He sold a
second time, to another publisher, one of the pieces
included in a collection of which Forster had bought
the rights for £70. The publishers brought an action
in London against Haydn, which the latter lost‡.

* *Lettres de Mozart*, French translation by H. de Curzon, p. 533.
For Elssler, see Pohl, *Joseph Haydn*, Vol. I, pp. 268 ff.

† ' The word *Laudon* will help the sales more than ten finales ' he
wrote on 10th April 1783. Nohl, *Musiker-Briefe*, p. 92. The name of
the Field-Marshal Baron von Laudon (1717-1790) was very popular
in Austria at the time.

‡ The collection in question comprised six trios, six sonatas, and
eight symphonies. *Forster and Son* were the principal proprietors of
Haydn's works in England. They published no less than one hundred
and twenty-nine compositions, of which eighty-two were symphonies.

Before taxing him with avarice, it is only just to take into consideration the narrow circumstances in which he had lived for so long, and to remember that as long as he stayed with the Esterhazy family he paid with his liberty for the material security of his existence. The man who had added lustre to his art and· had rejoiced all Europe with his melodies died in the modest position of a retired tradesman.

From Paris Haydn received in 1781 a proof of admiration which he greatly appreciated. Le Gros, conductor of the *Concert Spirituel,* wrote to congratulate him on the success of his *Stabat Mater,* of which four performances had just been given in a kind of competition with similar works by Pergolesi and by a Portuguese monk, Father Vito. In the name of French musicians, he invited Haydn to send all his new works to France, where they would be published ' to his great advantage '*. It was not, however, for the *Concert Spirituel,* but for the rival enterprise, called the *Concert de la Loge Olympique,* that Haydn wrote six of his larger symphonies in 1784. Le Gros, it appears, knew none of his vocal works except the *Stabat Mater* and was surprised that he should confine himself to instrumental composition, which, according to the ideas of the time in France, was considered of secondary importance. Moreover, his letter does not seem to have contained any invitation to go to Paris, for when Haydn was free to visit France, some years later, he did not think of doing so. Why should he have gone there? He could not pose as a writer of opera, after Gluck, Piccinni, Sacchini; to have presented himself only as a symphonist, like Eichner or Cannabich, would have assured him a reception unworthy of his merit; to shine in

* Of the letter from Le Gros there exists only a summary, which Haydn himself gave in a letter to Artaria. The conductor of the *Concert Spirituel* probably did not say that the prize went to the *Stabat Mater* of Pergolesi, and that to ensure the success of Haydn's, he had thought it necessary to cut it down from thirteen parts to ten, and to divide it into sections, which were separated on the programme by other works.

drawing-rooms, to mix in the intrigues which per-
petuated the quarrel of the 'Gluckists' and the
'Piccinnists', and to take part in the disputes of the
philosophic set, were not to his taste. Too entirely
devoted to his profession to accustom himself to the
manners of a society which was essentially 'literary',
good *Papa Haydn* would have confirmed the followers
of Voltaire in their scornful opinion that it was impossible to be at the same time a musician and a man of
intelligence.

It remains certain that although Haydn did not seek
to make personal acquaintances in Parisian musical
circles, he yet thought their approbation desirable. He
despatched direct to Paris many other compositions,
besides the symphonies for the *Loge Olympique*. The
score of *La Vera Costanza*, partly in his own handwriting
and partly copied, which is now in the Library of
the Conservatoire, and which came from the old Italian
theatre, was sent to Paris for public performance. It
was actually given—entirely without success—on 21st
January 1791, in a French translation, under the title
of *Laurette**.

In Spain, too, Haydn's instrumental works had
many warm admirers, including Boccherini, who
formally inscribes himself by a personal letter. Yriarte
gave expression to their enthusiasm in a canto of his
poem on music. A material proof of this admiration
reached Haydn in 1785, when a Canon of Cadiz re-
quested him to write a set of pieces to illustrate the
Seven Words of the Saviour on the Cross, to be performed during the services in Holy Week. The spon-
taneity of this homage added to its value.

Without any other effort than industry and perse-
verance, with no other advertisement than the discreetly

---

* It is natural to suppose that there was some connection between
this translation and the arrival at Esterhaz in May 1790 of a ' French
master ', which Haydn mentions in one of his letters to Frau von Genzinger. See Karajan, p. 74.

worded appeals of the publishers, without canvassing other than letters to princely subscribers and the customary dedications, Haydn's works became known more and more widely and his fame steadily increased. The time was approaching when he was to leave his tranquil retreat by the shores of the Neusiedler See, and at sixty years of age to enter the great world and taste the joys of popular triumph.

* *

The death of Prince Nicolas Esterhazy, on 28th September 1790, was the event which changed Haydn's destiny. For twenty-eight years he had served this ' excellent and magnificent ' prince, to whom, in spite of the fetters of a pseudo-slavery, he was so greatly attached that he wished to ' live and die ' with him. Prince Paul Anton, heir to the estates, had no taste for music, and one of his first cares was to disband the musicians, retaining only a little group, the players of wind-instruments, for music at the hunt and in the open air. Under Nicolas Esterhazy's will, Haydn received an annual pension of a thousand gulden. In dismissing him, Prince Anton increased this amount by four hundred gulden, on condition that the recipient should continue to bear the name of his *Kapellmeister*, and remain thus nominally attached to him, though he was left entirely free to use his time and his talent as he pleased.

As early as 1787, Haydn had thought of going to Naples on the invitation of King Ferdinand IV. This project, which recalls his old desire for a journey to Italy, was not realized when he left Esterhaz. The skill of a concert-organizer decided it otherwise. Scarcely had Haydn settled down in a house on the Wasserkunst-Bastei, one of the outer boulevards of Vienna, looking over the rows of chestnuts planted along the embankment, when a man called to see him, saying ' I am Salomon, of London. I have come to fetch you.'

Johann Peter Salomon (1745-1815), a native of
Bonn, and formerly violinist to the Elector of Cologne,
had left this post in 1765, and after staying in various
German towns and in Paris, had settled in London in
1781, where he appeared as a soloist on the violin and
viola, as member of a quartet, and as conductor of an
orchestra. Since 1786, he had been organizing subscription concerts, for which he secured the assistance
of prominent performers and composers. He happened
to be in Cologne when he heard of the death of Nicolas
Esterhazy. He hurried to Vienna at full speed, resolved
to bring to a satisfactory conclusion the negotiations
with Haydn, vainly initiated some years before by the
publisher Bland. This time the matter was soon settled.
Under their agreement, Haydn undertook to go to
London, and there to compose an opera for the impresario Gallini, and six symphonies and twenty other
pieces for Salomon, which the latter would conduct at
twenty concerts. His fee was to be £300 for the opera,
and a similar amount for the symphonies, with £200
for the copyright of these works, and another £200
for the twenty other compositions. He received, in
addition, the promise of a benefit concert, the minimum
receipts from which were guaranteed at £200. Salomon
deposited five thousand gulden in a Viennese bank as
security, and advanced five hundred gulden to Haydn
for the expenses of the journey.

When, on the eve of his departure, the master visited
the King of Naples, who had come to Vienna for the
triple wedding of three of his children with three
Austrian Archdukes and Archduchesses, and who had
asked for some music for the *lira**, Ferdinand at first
appeared very ill-pleased at the engagement. However,
when the first ill-humour passed, he became once more
the 'kind prince', made Haydn promise to go to

* The *lira* or *archiviola* was a kind of *viola da gamba* which, like the
theorbo or archlute, was provided with one or more low strings stretched
outside the neck.

Naples on his return from England, and gave him, in
addition to the usual gold snuff-box, a letter of introduction to the Neapolitan ambassador in London.

For a man whose whole life had been lived within
the compass of a few square miles, the journey to
England assumed the proportions of a great adventure.
It may even have appeared thus to Haydn's friends,
fearful to see him carry out, so late in life, so bold a
resolution. Mozart, who remembered his own pere-
grinations, and who thought Haydn poorly equipped
to face similar experiences on account of his ignorance
of foreign languages, was one of those who displayed
the greatest uneasiness. It was noted afterwards that
on bidding farewell to Haydn he seemed disturbed
and secretly afraid. The two friends, in actual fact,
never met again, but it was the younger for whom
death was already waiting.

Haydn and Salomon left Vienna on Wednesday,
15th December 1790, travelling via Munich, Bonn,
Brussels, and Calais. A modern painter has attempted
to perpetuate the memory of this journey, picturing
Haydn in strange garments and in a theatrical attitude
on the deck of a ship, where fair travellers show signs
of terror and a storm rages with a great flash of lightning tearing through thick clouds*. The truth of the
matter is that, although hindered at first by lack of
wind, the crossing took place in less than nine hours
without any untoward incident whatever. On arriving
in London, Haydn went to stay with Bland, the publisher, whom he already knew, and a few days later he
settled at 18 Great Pulteney Street, in rooms which
Salomon had procured for him near his own. The
master and his manager took their principal meal together and made together such visits as were judged
useful for their success.

* There are many reproductions of this picture. We shall only mention the one contained in the illustrated biography of Haydn by Leopold
Schmidt.

According to contemporary records, England was
at that time, as C. F. Pohl has depicted it*, ' an
isle full of song', where every day saw some new concert, musical society, or theatrical enterprise. It was
said, in jest, that John Bull, absorbed until then in
material pleasures, wanted to make up for lost time
by a sudden, immoderate, and undiscriminating in-
dulgence in music. Haydn's name was familiar to the
London public long before his journey. Several of his
symphonies had been given at concerts; amateurs
bought his quartets and sonatas; and several fragments
of his operas had been used in musical medleys made
up of airs taken from all kinds of works†. No great
skill on Salomon's part was required to ensure that
Haydn, from the moment of his landing, should
become the centre of interest of all musical, or would-be
musical, London. The Austrian ambassador introduced him, at his receptions, as a national celebrity;
the Neapolitan ambassador, as a *protégé* of his master.
He was invited to a ' Drawing-room ' at St. James's
Palace, to the Lord Mayor's Banquet at the Guildhall,
and to the celebrations at Oatlands in honour of the
marriage of the Duke of York to a Prussian Princess.
The *Academy of Ancient Music*, the *Anacreontic Society*,
the *Ladies' Concerts*, and all the musical associations,
wished to have the honour of entertaining him, and to
let him hear their best music and their best performers,
together with his own symphonies, quartets, and the
cantata *Ariadne in Naxos*. The reverse of the medal
was that he was sometimes obliged to listen to very
bad music, or even—what was still more unpleasant—

* In his two volumes entitled *Mozart in London* and *Haydn in
London*.

† In 1789 an opera, *The Prophet*, was staged at Covent Garden, for
which the music was drawn from works by Haydn, Pleyel, Grétry,
Anfossi, Cimarosa, Purcell, etc. In the same year an oratorio was
performed, *The Triumph of Truth*, for which Arnold had made up the
score by combining pieces by Purcell, Handel, Orme, Haydn, Corelli,
Jommelli, and Sacchini.

to horrible arrangements and travesties of his best works.

As soon as Salomon's series of concerts began, the enthusiasm of the British dilettanti exhausted all means of expression. On one occasion a listener snatched from Haydn, almost by force, as a souvenir, the worthless snuff-box he carried that day in his pocket, and had it enshrined, like a precious relic, in a silver coffer, ornamented with lyres and other symbols and Latin inscriptions. On another occasion, a hosier, carried away by his admiration, had made in his workshops, as an offering to the master, six pairs of socks with a design showing the notation of six of his melodies. There were many instances of artists who asked him for sittings: his portrait was painted three times during his first visit to London, twice during the second. The famous Dr. Burney, the oracle of musical criticism in England, dedicated a poem to him. He had so many invitations to dinner that, out of regard for his health, he was obliged to make it a rule to accept only those from titled people. All these things flattered Haydn greatly, and consoled him a little for the terribly expensive cost of living, of which he complained in his private letters.

The first concert took place on 11th March 1791, in the Hall at Hanover Square. The orchestra, conducted by Salomon, numbered thirty-five to forty instrumentalists. Haydn presided at the clavier in the performance of his symphony, which was placed, as he had insisted, at the beginning of the second part of the programme. The adagio was encored—a rare thing then in England. Haydn's success was brilliant and was renewed at each of the following concerts. The benefit concert, provided for on his engagement, took place on 16th May. The receipts touched £350, exceeding by £150 the guaranteed minimum. On the 30th of the same month ' on the request of several distinguished patrons ', Haydn conducted a supple-

mentary concert for the first performance in London of
the *Seven Words of Christ*.

In the theatre things did not happen quite so for-
tunately. The impresario, Gallini, for whom it was
stipulated in the contract that an opera should be
composed, had difficulty in his negotiations with the
English authorities for the right to produce Italian
opera on the newly-reconstructed stage of the King's
Theatre in the Haymarket. The Prince of Wales sup-
ported Gallini, but the King, prejudiced in favour of a
rival enterprise, did not seem disposed to allow the
simultaneous use of two theatres for opera. It was therefore in another form, and under the title *Entertainments
of Music and Dancing*, that the performances at the
Haymarket began on 26th March 1791. The caste,
as engaged by Gallini, included Davide, the tenor,
Vestris, the ballet-master, Salomon as conductor, and
Haydn as composer. Several short works of his were
actually given: a cantata written for Davide, a ' hunting
symphony ' accompanied by a *tableau vivant*, another
symphony in the tragic style, some overtures, quartets,
airs, and duets composed and arranged with Italian
words, and a chorus which, by a strange mingling of
two vocabularies, was called a 'Catch Italien'*. But the
opera, *Orfeo ed Eurydice*, with an Italian libretto, which
Haydn went into the country to write during the summer of 1791, was never put on—a disappointment
which Haydn felt keenly, and which made him abandon
the score unfinished.

In the same season, the University of Oxford conferred upon him the degree of Doctor of Music,
honoris causa. In acknowledgement of this honour,
Haydn went to Oxford, where three concerts, each

---

* The *Catch*, an old and popular form of English vocal music, is a
composition for several voices, with a comic effect predominating, produced by the entrances and combinations of the parts and words. See
Grove, *Dictionary of Music*, 2nd edition, Vol. I, pp. 481 ff., articles
Catch and *Catch Club*.

including one of his symphonies, were given in his presence on 6th, 7th, and 8th July 1791, under the direction of Dr. Hayes. As a memento of the conferring of the degree, which took place on the 8th, with music, speeches, and recitations of Latin and English verse, Haydn later sent to the University the manuscript of a canon cancrizans for three voices.

Obviously Salomon's first object in bringing to London the *Kapellmeister* of the Princes Esterhazy was not to gratify his vanity. He was a concert pro-moter, and his chief business was to hold his own in the struggle with a formidable rival, the *Professional Concerts.* The directors of this organization could think of nothing better, the following season, than to bring from Strassburg, where he was in charge of the cathedral choir, Ignaz Pleyel, Haydn's pupil, then very popular —principally, be it noted, with the ladies. By means of clamorous or pointed advertisement the attempt was made to place him on an equal footing with his master. From vanity or greed, rather than from envy, Pleyel acquiesced in this course, and lent himself to under-hand dealings which might have been detrimental to Haydn, and which actually did injure him in some respects. At first the two musicians displayed towards one another only those friendly feelings which their former relationship should have warranted sincere. Living in the same street, they were often seen dining at the same table or in company at the same entertain-ments. However, when the directors of the *Professional Concerts* announced a series of twelve concerts, at each of which a new symphony of Pleyel's would be per-formed—the latter, a tireless and prolific worker, had brought with him from Strassburg a whole cargo of music—Salomon, in self-defence, had to promise at his own six concerts six hitherto unpublished sym-phonies by Haydn, who set to work, without inter-mission, on their composition. ' My eyes have suffered' he said in a letter to his friends in Vienna ' and I have written many a time all through the night, but with God's help, I shall get through it '. In addition to these symphonies he had to contribute to Salomon's programmes a concerto, a *divertissement*, a trio, and a chorus—*The Storm*—which won approval, because it was composed for English words by John Wolcot, the poet who boldly took as pseudonym the designation *Peter Pindar*.

The rivalry of the two concert enterprises held the public interest during the spring of 1792, from February to May. Having had some difficulty in considering as *virtuosi* two musicians who played no instruments, people eagerly came to stare at them and to applaud their works, if not to make intelligent comparisons. The directors tactfully affected an extreme politeness towards the two composers. No sooner had the *Professional Concerts* invited Haydn to come and hear one of his symphonies than Salomon hastened to pay Pleyel a similar courtesy. The public, greeting the pupil with acclamations, did not intend thereby to diminish the homage paid to the master.

Seen at a distance, there is something almost insulting in the readiness with which the crowd places on an equality the truly creative musician and the average composer. And the failure of the Londoners in 1792 has too many parallels for us to reproach them with it. At least they lavished on Haydn, until the end, both kindnesses and proofs of genuine admiration.

At length, however, serious fatigue followed from the overwork that had been imposed upon him. His letters of March and April 1792 are full of complaints which so industrious a man would not have made without cause. ' Not a day, no, not a single day passes without work, and I shall thank God when he allows me to leave London. . . . I am tired out, exhausted with so much toil, and I long for rest with all my heart. . . .' He left at the end of June 1792 and took the shortest route for Vienna, giving up the visit which he had

thought of making to Berlin. On passing through
Bonn, he was entertained to lunch by the musical staff
of the Elector, among whom he may have noticed
Beethoven, who was to rejoin him and ask for lessons
a few months later.

At Vienna Haydn found peace once more, with
old habits and old friends, although Mozart, the
greatest, the youngest, and one of the dearest, was
missing. He also found his wife, who was waiting
patiently for him, and who had chosen in a peaceful
suburb a pleasant little house and garden, where she
proposed to live comfortably 'when she was a widow'.
Haydn liked the house. He bought it and added another story to it. But, contrary to his wife's intentions,
it was he who inhabited it as a widower, after his second
journey to London*.

During his long absence he had remained nominally
attached to the household of Prince Esterhazy. When,
after eighteen months' rest, Haydn allowed himself
to be tempted afresh by Salomon's offers, he was again
obliged to ask permission of his 'master'. He next
set to work to find a travelling companion—a matter
of prudence as well as of pleasure and convenience. At
first, it is said, he thought of taking his new pupil,
Beethoven. Soon he fixed on his copyist, Johann
Elssler, who could make himself useful in many ways.
They started on 19th January 1794 and arrived in
London on 4th February.

As on the former occasion, Haydn contributed new
works to each of the twelve concerts given by Salomon;
and he reaped the same success, the same honours,
the same profits, as before. He had left in England
friends and admirers eager to make him welcome.
Though the first access of curiosity had calmed down,
a more serious and solid interest henceforth dominated

* Haydn's house in the Kleine Steingasse, Windmühle, now called
Haydngasse, changed hands several times, without being altered ex-
ternally. In 1839 a tablet was put up with the words *Zum Haydn*.

the public. The Court and the royal family were more
regardful of his presence, more appreciative of his
merit. After a reception at the Duke of York's a formal
proposal was made that he should settle permanently
in England. But Haydn, warmly attached to his own
country and to the Esterhazy family, rejected the offer,
saying that he was bound by ties of gratitude to his
former masters. Prince Anton had just died, and his
successor, Prince Nicolas, who seemed disposed to
reorganize the old musical staff, was pressing Haydn
to return. As soon as the period of his engagement
with Salomon came to an end, the master left London,
on 15th August 1795*.

In the record of his journeys which he made later
for Griesinger, Haydn mentioned that the total number of pages of music which he wrote during his two
visits to England amounted to seven hundred and
sixty-eight. As against this figure, he stated no less
exactly the amount of his gains, which he estimated, in
Austrian money, at twenty-four thousand gulden. It was
not a fortune, but it gave him all that he desired—the
assurance of a peaceful life in the twilight of his days.

* *

The intention attributed to the new prince of re-
storing the musical luxury of his house was never
carried out; and, indeed, Haydn, tired and prematurely
aged, might never have had the energy to recruit,
train, and direct a numerous body of musicians. But,
always industrious and faithful to what he considered
his duty, he continued to pay honour, by his work, to
the prince whose guest he again was at Eisenstadt
each summer. In 1797, Nicolas Esterhazy increased
his pension by three hundred florins, then by six hundred in 1806, which brought up the total sum to two
thousand three hundred florins a year.

* The diary kept by Haydn on his second journey was published in
1909 by J. Engl.

Mozart and Gluck were dead. Beethoven, who had
barely reached his thirtieth year, had as yet only produced work in his ' first manner ', in which few musicians divined the future master. Haydn, ' loaded with
laurels ', seemed the sole musical hero of Vienna and
all Germany. Shortly after his return from London,
his compatriots had given him a pleasant surprise, by
placing his bust on a peninsula of the Leitha, near to
his native village, Rohrau. Each of his new works was
received with respectful enthusiasm. On 18th December
1795, at the Redoutensaal, he gave the Viennese an
opportunity of hearing three of the symphonies written
for Salomon. On the same occasion, Beethoven, who
had little reason to be satisfied with Haydn's very
inadequate lessons*, showed him all the deference due
from a grateful pupil, and played his first or second
piano concerto. Although he complained that his
strength was ebbing, Haydn did not relax his zeal in
composition. Between 1796 and 1802, he produced
four ' Grand Masses ', a *Te Deum*, several collections
of quartets, trios, and sonatas, an entirely new version
of the *Seven Words of Christ*, a few songs, and a cantata, in addition to the two great works of his old age,
The Creation and *The Seasons*.

Not content to acclaim in him the master of symphony, his friends had for some time been urging him to
attempt the oratorio form again. His *Ritorno di Tobia*
was not enough to put him in the first rank of oratorio
composers, and Handel's masterpieces, which he had
heard in England, must have made Haydn also wish
to produce some examples in this style.   Not long
before, in London, Salomon had given him an English
poem by Lidley, a distant imitation of Milton and
the Bible. A Viennese librarian, Gottfried van Swieten,
undertook to arrange it and translate it into German.
This was *The Creation* (*Die Schöpfung*), of which two
private performances were given on 29th and 30th

* See J. Chantavoine, *Beethoven*, pp. 61 ff.

April 1798, at the Prince Schwartzenberg's, and the
first public performance in the Nationaltheater, on
Haydn's nameday, 19th March 1799. Recently re-
conciled with the *Tonkünstler-Societät*, the master
consented to conduct a performance of his work, which
he did at Buda in the presence of the Archduke Joseph.
In the course of the next few years, *The Creation* was
given in London, Lisbon, St. Petersburg, and Paris.
Bonaparte, then First Consul, was going to the opera
to hear it when he escaped the explosion of the infernal
machine in the rue Saint Nicaise. Haydn's score had
been taken to France by the pianist Steibelt. Translated
by J. A. de Ségur, and sung by Garat, Chéron, Mme.
Barbier-Valbonne, and Mlle. Chevalier (the future
Mme. Branchu), with a chorus of fifty voices and an
orchestra of a hundred and fifty-six performers, it
made a profound impression on the French public.
To commemorate the event a medal was struck, engraved by Gatteaux and bearing the effigy of Haydn.

The applause which everywhere greeted *The Creation* had not died down when van Swieten proposed
to Haydn a German adaptation of Thomson's poem
The Seasons. The master hesitated some time before
allowing himself to be convinced. He thought himself
too old to undertake another great work. Scruples of
modesty held him back. The words, too, seemed to
him prosaic. However, his success, certain in advance,
was complete, both when the work was given at Prince
Schwartzenberg's on 24th and 27th April and 1st
May 1801, and when Haydn himself conducted it at
his benefit concert in the Redoutensaal on 29th May.

In the same hall, on 26th December 1800, he conducted for the last time in public one of his own
works, *The Seven Words of Christ*. Henceforward, he
declined all similar invitations. He was growing gradually weaker; work was becoming difficult for him.
Except for a few songs, which he sent to the Empress
of Russia, he composed nothing after *The Seasons*.

To complete his eighty-third string quartet, he took some phrases from one of his songs, entitled *Der Greis*, and he had them printed with his name and the words 'Hin ist alle meine Kraft; alt und schwach bin ich'* on the souvenir cards which he addressed to his friends.

In 1808, these friends wished to give him the pleasure of a last triumph. Salieri was conducting a performance of *The Creation*. They took him in a wheeled chair to the concert hall, where he was received by the public with warm applause. Haydn was extremely agitated from the beginning. When the splendid fortissimo broke forth ' And there was light', he rose, and pointing upwards, said ' It came from on high '. At the end of the first part, they had to take him into the midst of the enthusiastic demonstrations of the audience, who cheered him and pressed round to kiss his hands. He thanked them from the threshold with a gesture of benediction and farewell.

Haydn lived with his memories in the house on the Steingasse, where Elssler and one or two old servants looked after him. He was a widower. His two brothers —to each of whom he had left four thousand florins in his first will, dated 6th December 1801—were dead. He had seen his sisters, too, disappear, and his only relatives now were their children, his nephews and nieces, modest artisans, tailors, shoemakers, jewellers, whose names are mentioned with those of his servants, his neighbours, and the poor, in the sixty-three clauses of that same will†.

His last pupils were Ignaz von Seyfried (1776-1841), who was a conductor and a prolific composer; Sigismund Neukomm (1778-1858), who came from

* All my strength is spent; I am old and weak.

† The text of it was published by Nohl, *Musiker-Briefe*, pp. 161 ff. Six weeks before his death, in 1808, Haydn replaced this will by a new one, as it had become ineffective through the deaths of the beneficiaries or by his own change of purpose.

Salzburg, where his musical education had been begun by Michael Haydn; and Franz Lessel (1780-1838), a doctor of medicine and a composer, son of a *Kapellmeister* to Prince Czartorisky. His disciples and admirers dedicated their works to him. Beethoven offered him, in 1796, his three pianoforte sonatas (op. 2). Neukomm, in 1798, composed for him a *New Year Greeting* for four voices. The Abbé Maximilian Stadler (1748-1833), a famous organist, wrote an andante for string quartet, in which he used Haydn's theme 'Hin ist alle meine Kraft', for the upper part. In 1806 Albrechtsberger dedicated to him his canons on the words 'Solatium miseris, socios habuisse dolorum'. The verses on *The Creation* which the celebrated Wieland wrote about this time are supposed to have been one of the compliments which the master most appreciated.

Besides, he received visits. The strangers admitted to greet him found him seated in a big armchair, carefully dressed in the old style, in an embroidered vest and a coat of fine brown cloth, with breeches of black silk, white stockings, buckled shoes, a frilled shirt, a white cravat, and a long wig curled, powdered, and reaching to within an inch of his eyebrows; on his finger, the ring from the King of Prussia; and near him, on a table, his hat, stick, and gloves. He was of small stature, but solidly built, the body a little too big for the limbs. His face, freckled and marked with small-pox, was massive and strongly featured, the nose too big and deformed by a polypus, the chin heavy, and the lower lip prominent. Lavater, judging from a silhouette, found in his profile a combination of vulgarity and intelligence, displeasing at first sight, but corrected by the good nature of the smile*. When he

* Emil Vogel, in Peters' *Jahrbuch* for 1898, gives a list of ninety-one portraits of Haydn. Sixteen of them were reproduced in Henri Marcel's article *L'Iconographie d'Haydn*, which appeared in the monthly *S.I.M.* of 15th January 1910.

was in a good mood, he would get his secretary or his
valet to bring in the relics of his career which he took
pleasure in displaying to his visitors—the snuff-boxes
given by kings, the medal from the French musicians
and that from the Philharmonic Society of St. Petersburg, on which were the words *Orpheo redivivo*, the
watch given to him at Eisenstadt in 1797 by Nelson
in exchange for the pen with which he had just finished
a manuscript, diplomas from academies or musical
societies of Paris, Amsterdam, and Stockholm, and
one from the citizens of Vienna, received in 1803. On
the walls, he would point out canons of his own composition, framed and glazed, saying ' I am not rich
enough to buy beautiful pictures, so I have made for
myself a decoration that everyone cannot procure '.
He grew animated when talking, ransacked his memories, and delighted to tell the innocuous jests of his
youth—a burlesque serenade which he organized one
evening in the streets of Vienna with comrades whom
he directed to play each a different tune, taking to his
heels first of them all when this hubbub had angered
all the inhabitants of the district—or the trick he
played on his wife when she was watching over him
during an illness, and when he succeeded in sending
her out of the room, so that he might hastily get up
and note down a sonata composed during the excite-
ment of the fever*. At other times, his natural gaiety
suddenly abandoned him; he grieved over the useless-
ness of his old age, and over the loss of his memory;
sometimes he wept. Iffland saw him thus, and withdrew on a sign from his servant, who knew the senile
sensibility of his master.

Peacefully, Haydn grew familiar with the idea of
death, which the strength of his religious faith enabled
him to accept without fear. ' I am no longer of any use

---

* The works of Dies, Griesinger, and Carpani, the names of which
are given at the end of this volume, abound in anecdotes drawn from
this source.

in this world ' he would say; ' I have only to wait like a child for the time when God calls me to himself '. The shadow which darkened his last days was his grief for the misfortunes of Austria. On 10th May 1809, the French arrived at the gates of Vienna. Haydn conquered his first momentary fear, and reassured his household. He took to his bed, however, almost at once, and the last visit he received was that of an officer in Napoleon's army, who sat down at his piano and sang to him Uriel's song from *The Creation*, ' Mit Würd' und Hoheit angetan '. Haydn, without speaking, embraced this enemy of his country and admirer of his genius, whose homage in such circumstances was peculiarly touching. A few days later, on 26th May, he wished to get up and was led to his piano, where he played three times in succession, like an urgent prayer, the *Austrian Hymn*, which he had composed some time before for the Emperor Francis. His weakness rapidly increased. He fell asleep on 31st May 1809, at about one o'clock in the morning.

HIS WORKS

OPERAS

IN repeating to Artaria the compliments which he had just received from Le Gros on the performance in Paris of his *Stabat Mater*, Haydn added regretfully ' If only the French could know my operetta *L'Isola Disabitata* and my last opera *La Fedelta Premiata*! I am sure such works have never yet been heard in Paris, perhaps not even in Vienna '. In which he showed a considerable misapprehension as to the merits of his dramatic work, and a naive ignorance of the productions of other writers. The letter to Artaria is dated 27th May 1781. By that date, Gluck had given in Paris his immortal lyric tragedies, Piccinni his *Atys* and *Iphigénie en Tauride*, and Grétry the better part of his work. Nearer home, at Munich, Mozart's *Idomeneo* had just been played, a work in which he already dared to challenge the old *opera seria*. But there are some havens so sheltered that, even in the most violent storms, the breakers do not reach them. Haydn, at Esterhaz, was living in such a port, and it is no reflection upon him that he did not know what happened in the outside world, still less that he did not compete with his contemporaries in the field of drama. Even had he wished to do so, had his genius given him the necessary power, he would have been unable to attempt it. The nature, proportions, and style of his operas were dictated by circumstance. In the first place, he must please his prince. Next, he must work within the limitations of his surroundings and the resources of a mediocre company. Haydn, moreover, never complained of the narrow means at his disposal. The pupil of Porpora, brought up in the old traditions of Italian song, submissively followed the models, concerning which no doubt ever arose in his mind.

Among his works there were five Italian operas
written for the entertainments at Eisenstadt, and eleven
for those at Esterhaz. Of the first series only fragments
remain. Of the second series, all the scores exist, either
in autographed manuscripts, or in copies, but not
without gaps. Most of these belong to the type of
dramma giocoso which Prince Nicolas favoured, and
with an eye to which most of his singers were recruited.
Lo Speziale is a humorous piece, in the comic vein
which was then in vogue, and which we find
again in *L'Incontro Improviso*. *L'Infedelta Delusa* is
described as 'burletta per musica' and *Orlando
Paladino* as 'dramma eroi-comico'. *Le Pescatrici* and
L'Isola Disabitata come nearer in style to the serious
'dramma eroico' *Armida*, which Haydn distinguished,
at the time of its composition, as his best work 'up to
the present '.

Neither Haydn nor his rivals sought out unpublished libretti. Custom sanctioned the seizure by any
musician of any poem. For *Lo Speziale*, *Le Pescatrici*
and *Il Mondo della Luna*, Haydn used libretti by
Goldoni, which had already been set to music by
Vincenzo Pallavicini or Domenico Fischietti, Bertoni
or Galuppi. His friend, the tenor, Friberth, manufac-
tured the words of *L'Incontro Improviso* by recasting
Dancourt's libretto of *La Rencontre Imprévue*, which
Gluck had given, in Vienna itself, in 1765. The words
of *La Vera Costanza*, by Francesco Puttini and Pietro
Travaglia, and those of *Orlando Paladino* and *Armida*,
of which the authors were Nunziato Porta and Durandi,
respectively, had all been set by Anfossi. Once only,
Haydn had recourse to a poem by his old neighbour
and helper, Metastasio, *L'Isola Disabitata*, which had
already been used by Bonno, Scarlatti, Naumann,
Traetta, and Jommelli.

A birthday, an anniversary, a wedding or a reception, were occasions celebrated at Esterhaz by the
composition and performance of new operas. More

than once, the *Kapellmeister* was obliged to prepare his scores with a haste that is shown in the writing of the manuscripts. By the nature of their origin, as entertainments of a day, these scores were condemned to obscurity, and to an ephemeral life, which the efforts of Haydn or his friends rarely succeeded in extending. The German translations of *L'Incontro Improviso* and *La Vera Costanza*, made by a musician of Count Erdödy for that nobleman's use, and those of *La Fedelta Premiata* and *Orlando Paladino* were represented during Haydn's lifetime in the smaller theatres in Vienna, Pressburg, Graz, Brünn, and in some towns of northern Germany. It was on the concert platform, or as it was then said, in 'Academy', that the music was given of *L'Isola Disabitata* at Vienna, 1785; of *Armida* at Vienna, 1797, and at Turin, 1808; and the unfinished *Orfeo ed Euridice*, at Konigsberg, 1808. An unfortunate attempt was made in 1791 to popularize *La Vera Costanza* in Paris, translated into French, or rather, adapted, by Dubuisson under the title of *Laurette**. The only performance given at the 'Théâtre de Monsieur' was heard with a patient calm which broke down before the end. 'The name of Haydn' writes an anonymous critic 'has strengthened popular opinion in favour of this music. We see the fine technique of the master in several pleasant melodies. However, the severer critics do not find in it that lively originality which distinguishes his instrumental music. It seems

* Dubuisson was the author of a few libretti and the translator of Paisiello's *King Theodore*, which was played in 1786 at the courts of Fontainebleau and Versailles. In his arrangement of *La Vera Costanza*, the order is changed, serious cuts are made in the finale of the first act (which is moved to the end of Act II), and the overture is replaced by that of *Armida*. *Laurette* was performed in Paris on 21st January 1791. The score was printed in Paris by Imbault. To this translation we owe the existence of a manuscript of *La Vera Costanza* found among the scores of the old Italian theatre, sold in 1789. This is almost entirely in Haydn's own hand, and dated by him, on the last page 1785, and on the title page 1788. This manuscript is now in the library of the Paris Conservatoire.

that the freedom-loving genius of the famous symphonist loses all its power under the yoke of words. The
greatest of composers, when he commands instruments
to express his ideas, sinks to mediocrity when the poet
commands him in his turn'*. A short time after,
Reichardt expressed exactly the same opinion, in
Berlin on the translation of *Orlando Paladino*. ' I think
the best critics agree with me in preferring Haydn's
instrumental to his vocal music. Perhaps his genius is
impeded by words. Many singers are dissatisfied with
his manner of writing for the voice. The theatre is not
his province'†.

' The best critics ' of the twentieth century would
see nothing to alter in these last words‡. The conventional formalism of the school of Hasse is nowhere
compensated in Haydn's operas by an interesting
development of the orchestral parts, such as we might
expect to find, at least occasionally, in the work of one
of the creators of the quartet and the symphony. If,
on the other hand, knowing his life, we take care not
to expect from him the accents of great tragedy, we
must not imagine that his good-humour and equable
temperament will provoke him to unexpected out-
bursts in the comic vein. Lively comedy is a style which
Haydn cannot, will not, or dare not use. Charming
melodies succeed one another soberly in a serio-comic
vein, and when greater liveliness is needed, we find
little motifs breaking in, like a flight of chaffinches,
light, babbling, careless, similar to one another, escaped
as though out of a cage, from the rondos of his sonatas

* *Le Moniteur*, 24th January 1791.

† *Berlinische Musikzeitung*, 1805, No. 39: quoted by Wendschuh,
Über Jos. Haydn's Opern, p. 103.

‡ There has been an attempt in our own time to resurrect the opera
Lo Speziale: translated into German, and cut down by Dr. Hirsch-
feld from three acts to one, this little work was played in 1895 at Dresden, Hamburg, and at a charity concert in Vienna. The same opera
and the one-act opera *L'Isola Disabitata* were performed in Vienna in
1909, during the celebrations of the centenary of Haydn's death.

and the finales of his symphonies. Here is one of them from the first part of *La Vera Costanza:*

1

and its twin from the finale of the second act:

2

and, still from the same opera, this quartet:

3

which runs so freely and in such a dancing rhythm that the French adapter can see nothing better to do with it than to detach it from its vocal setting, and present it, almost without accompaniment, in the form of a *vaudeville* in three verses.

In making a selection of the more elaborate pieces —airs preceded by accompanied recitative, or grand finales of several movements, imitated from Piccinni or others—we still find this abundance of short and symmetrical melodies of cheerful rhythm, easy to remember, and so slightly attached to the words that they seem made in advance for a thousand other settings. All these might lead the reader to wonder whether Haydn would not have found his true dramatic model in the *Singspiel,* or German comic opera, which is equivalent to the French *vaudeville* or early light opera. He made one experiment in it* before he was bound by his obligations as *Kapellmeister* to the exclusive cult

* His operetta, *Der Neue Krumme Teufel,* which is lost, has been already referred to, p. 12. Of the two similar works which have been attributed to him, one, *Der Apfeldieb,* is a pastiche of airs by various composers; the other, *Die Hochzeit auf der Alm,* is by his brother Johann Michael.

of Italian opera. But it is idle to wonder what would
have happened if other events had shaped a man's life
and determined the direction of his activities. Besides,
Haydn's tardy and unimportant contributions to the
repertory of song* exist to prove that he had no special
bent nor any particular talent for vocal music. The
development of the *Lied* runs parallel in Germany with
that of lyric poetry, and there is nothing to indicate
that Haydn was interested in either. Again, his connection with a prince of decided tastes and despotic
temper left him neither the freedom to choose his work
nor the leisure to indulge his curiosity. In spite of his
excellent opinion of his own operas, which he confided
so ingenuously to Artaria in 1781, Haydn was too
modest and too clear-sighted not to realize the im-
possibility of rivalling, in this sphere, the young master
whose rise to fame he had witnessed, and whose sincere
admirer and devoted friend he gladly became. His
reply to a letter from Prag in 1787, asking him
to compose an opera for that city, where *Don Giovanni*
had just been given, does credit to his good sense as
well as to his good heart. ' You ask me ' he said ' for
comic light opera. Certainly, if you are willing to reserve for private use some vocal work of my composition. But if it is intended for performance in the theatre
at Prag, then I cannot serve you, for all my operas
are written for the special conditions of Esterhaz,
and could not produce elsewhere the effect I have cal-
culated upon for this setting. It would be otherwise if
I had the inestimable good fortune to be able to compose for your theatre upon a completely new libretto.
Though, there again, I should run too many risks, for
it would be difficult for anyone—no matter whom—
to equal the great Mozart. That is why I wish that all
music-lovers, especially the influential, could know
the inimitable works of Mozart with a profundity, a
musical knowledge, and a keen appreciation equal to

* His first songs appeared in 1781.

my own. Then the nations would compete for possession of such a treasure. Prag must hold fast so precious
a man—and reward him. For without that, the history of a great genius is a sad one, and gives posterity
little encouragement to follow the same course. That
is why so much fine and hopeful talent unfortunately
perishes. I am full of anger when I think that this
unique genius is not yet attached to a royal or imperial court. Forgive this outburst: I love the man
too much'*.

We have already heard of his dream of *Le Nozze
di Figaro* on returning from Vienna to Esterhaz†.

Apart from the theatre, Haydn's other secular vocal
works are not numerous, compared with his indefatigable labours in other directions. There are, in
addition to the songs, a few cantatas and Italian airs,
a German funeral ode on the death of the King of
Prussia, a burlesque German cantata on ' The Choice
of a *Kapellmeister*', written in Vienna for a ' merry
company of friends ' who used to meet at the Swan
Tavern, and the English chorus *The Storm*, which was
quickly translated into Italian. This chorus and the
scena entitled *Arianna a Naxos* show Haydn's talent
for vocal composition at its best. *Arianna a Naxos*,
which he used to call his ' dear Arianna ', was composed
in 1789, and became famous after the performances
given in London by the singer Pacchiarotti. Melodious
throughout and well suited to the voice, it consists of
two airs, preceded by an instrumental introduction
and a recitative, and connected by an obbligato recitative. According to usage in *opera seria* two successive
themes are opposed in the first air; one with a broadly-
stated melody:

* This letter, addressed to an official in Prag named Roth, was published for the first time by Niemtschek in his biography of Mozart, and
has often been reproduced by the historians of the two masters. Pohl
gives it in his *Joseph Haydn*, Vol. II, p. 225, and Nohl in his *Musiker-
Briefe*, p. 101.

† See above, p. 39, Letter to Frau von Genzinger.

the other in the key of the dominant, a little more animated, in form at least, if not in its general movement:

In the second part, or second air, Haydn attempts to convey passion. Ariadne, not seeing Theseus come, climbs a rock from which she sees the Greek ship disappearing across the sea. She gives vent to her despair in the conventional form of a recitative, a very tuneful larghetto ' a che morir vorrei ', and a presto which is unfortunately concluded by the orthodox common-place coda*.

In his chorus, *The Storm*, Haydn has traced out one of those musical pictures of which interesting examples are later found in his two great oratorios, and of which a few are already outlined in his operas. From the opening measures, the spectator is cast in the midst of a storm, in which time, syncopation, accidentals, discords, abrupt dynamic oppositions, all the colours spread on the palette of an eighteenth-century musician, are brought into play. The choir expresses its fear of the roaring of the winds by imitating their chromatic moaning (See page 70).

In the accompaniment compact phrases, built up one upon another, and a series of short rapid passages, represent the ceaseless drift of the clouds veiling the moon and rent by flashes of lightning. Powerful chords emphasize the chorus's cries of anguish. An *andante cantabile*, inviting the return to calm, interrupts the description of the storm, and is used again to form a quiet and harmonious conclusion to the work.

SACRED MUSIC

The contradiction between the purpose and the musical style which we find in most of the sacred music of the eighteenth century is explained first by their being often written without conviction, and secondly by the uniformity of the means of expression everywhere imposed by the vogue of Italian opera and of vocal virtuosity.

We cannot use the first argument to determine the

* *Arianna a Naxos*, translated into German, was orchestrated and touched up by Ernest Franck, who added vocal ornaments similar to those with which the Italian singers of the period were accustomed to burden the airs they interpreted. This edition was criticized by F. Spiro in the *Allgemeine Musikzeitung*, Berlin, 11th December 1885.

6

cause of the ' worldly ' character of Haydn's Church
music. It has long been recognized that the secu-
larity of his masses is as incontestable a fact as the
integrity of his faith*. The son of the Rohrau wagon-
maker had grown up in the tradition of a firm and open
faith, simple as that of a child, which he was fortunate
enough to keep unimpaired until his death. Evil be to
him who could think evil in reading the proofs of his
piety in the narratives of his visitors or in his own pages.

* These are the words used by Professor Bischof in an article in the
Niederrheinische Musikzeitung of 1858, which was quoted in the *Kirchen-*
musikalisches Jahrbuch of 1887, p. 52.

'You see' he said to the composer Schultz in 1770 'I rise early, and as soon as I am dressed, I kneel and pray to God and the Holy Virgin that all may go well with me again to-day. After a light breakfast, I sit down at the keyboard and begin to seek for ideas. If I come across something at once, work goes quickly and with little trouble. But when it does not go well, then I know that I have lost the heavenly favour through some sin, and I return to prayer until I feel myself forgiven.' * When he had completed a manuscript, he often wrote some devotional formula by way of signature, nor did he scruple to apply such terms even to his secular works. The words ' Laus deo et V. M.' are at the end of the comic opera *Lo Speziale*, and the score of the ' burletta' entitled *L'Infedelta Delusa* bears the inscription ' Laus omnipotenti Deo et Beatissimae Virgini Mariae'. Indeed, the initial invocation ' In nomine Domini' has been held to prove the authenticity of a cantata of which only an incomplete copy is in existence.

It can be proved abundantly that Haydn had the sincerest intentions in his religious compositions, therefore whatever renders them unsuitable for their purpose must be attributed to external causes.

Just as in the domain of dramatic music, we must first accuse ' the prince', who has been characterized by R. Schlect, an historian of Church music of the period, as one of the disruptive forces of Catholic art†. For all the composers whose livelihood was assured by employment at a court, the inevitable obligation to please the sovereign was everywhere of the first importance. How was it possible to continue to please him in church, unless by using the methods that succeeded elsewhere, which methods, being classed as the best, it seemed

---

* Schulz's account was published by Reichardt in the *Allgemeine Musikalische Zeitung* of Leipzig in the year 1800, p. 173. See Pohl, *Joseph Haydn*, Vol. II, p. 27.

† Schlecht, *Geschichte der Kirchenmusik*, pp. 144 ff.

unnecessary to set aside when it was a question of
'singing the praise of God'? To which we must add
that, as the same performers transferred their talents
and habits from the theatre to the chapel, there was
not much chance of maintaining a real separation between the two repertories. The only appreciable difference was that, in church, the composer had full liberty
to parade his learning. The concluding words of the
different parts of the mass, such as the various *amens*,
the words ' Cum Sancto Spiritu ' in the *Gloria*, and 'Et
vitam venturi saeculi' in the Creed, were occasions for
the writing of great fugues alternating with florid airs
and recitatives in the operatic style. When these works
had great musical value, they went to enrich an admirable stock of non-liturgical religious music, suitable
for the concert platform, of which the two unequal
peaks were reached, a century apart, by Bach's *Mass in
B minor*, and Beethoven's *Mass in D*. Haydn's great
Latin compositions should be classed in the category
of music suitable for the sacred concert.

Stollbrock asserts that the sacred works of Johann
Georg Reutter served as a model for his pupil. ' The
melodiousness of Haydn ' he says ' is the perfect development of that of Reutter.' It is a delicate and risky
matter to trace the influence of any school, particularly
when one can only point out very distant effects.
Haydn's most important compositions for the Church
belong to a period very remote from his sojourn in the
choir of St. Stephen's. Besides, Reutter's work, as it
is described in his biography, has many aspects. There
are great masses developed at much length and heavily
orchestrated, with motets loaded with *bravura* and
very difficult to perform, which this musician wrote to
show off the virtuosity of his wife, the singer Theresa
Holzhauser. There were also compositions *a capella*
which, we are assured, ' have a great and solemn beauty '.
An anecdote about one of his masses will show their
significance from the liturgical aspect. Reutter was

growing old and desired to obtain permission from the Empress to use one of the Court carriages. He conceived the idea of writing the *Dona nobis* of a mass upon a rhythm imitated from the descriptive line of Vergil:

Quadrupedante putrem sonitu quatit ungula campum.

Maria Theresa noticed the strange rhythm of the piece and questioned the author, who explained that the fatigue of old age made him wish that he need no longer go on foot. The equipage which the Empress placed at his disposal gave its name to the work, which attained a brief popularity under the title of *Schimmelmesse*, or ' the mass of the white horses '.*

This is only an isolated example of the decline of the religious spirit in musical composition. The ordinance published in 1738 by Joseph II to limit the use of instrumental music in church to the great festivals, coming, as it did, at the moment when this decline was at its worst, has seemed to certain historians an act inspired by the best intentions. This interpretation arises from the isolation of the edict from its context and from other measures enacted by the Emperor against the liberty of the Catholic faith. The order forbade the celebration of more than one Mass at a time in any church except St. Stephen's, where three might be recited. It declared that orchestral music should be permitted only in the imperial chapel, in the cathedral when the archbishop was officiating, and in other churches on stated days. The introduction into the service of arty hymns or chants in the German language, which could be sung by the people, was also forbidden. Such a decree can be interpreted neither as the echo of ancient orders of the Council, since fallen into disuse, nor as a forerunner of the recent *Motu proprio* of Pius X. The Emperor Joseph II cared

* A similar anecdote is related of one of the masses of Josquin Deprés.

no more for the æsthetic than for the liturgical point
of view. But he carried into every department his tire-
some mania for making the greatest possible number
of regulations, his passion for economy, and his anti-
clericalism. Did he not make war upon the religious
orders, suppress more than six hundred monasteries
in his dominions, selling by auction all their possessions,
including sacred objects and works of art, forbid students to go to Rome to take the courses at the German
College, prohibit pilgrimages, and put a stop to votive
offerings? And did he not carry his petty economies
to the point of prohibiting the use at funerals of silver
candlesticks, because it kept a precious metal out of
circulation, and of coffins, ' for which the planks employed were a complete loss'.* The presence of an
orchestra in the choir was, in his eyes, less an offence
against religious austerity than a sign of costly and
superfluous luxury. And if he found ' too many notes '
in a mass, or in other music—as for example in *Il
Seraglio*†—it was not out of regard for taste or convention, but very literally from the point of view of extravagance and the expense of performance.

The very excess and folly of such a tyranny caused
its violent manifestations to miscarry. As regards music,
no useful reform could result from it. After a brief
period of disturbance, the old habits were quickly
resumed, and their abuses flourished more than ever.
Haydn was at Esterhaz when the imperial decree was
issued, and there was no need for him to concern himself with it. After he settled in Vienna, the repeal of
Joseph II's decree by the new emperor, Leopold,
restored full liberty to musicians. Haydn was one of
the first to take advantage of it, composing in 1790
the most heavily orchestrated of his masses, the one
which received the name of *Missa in tempore belli*, or
the 'Drum Mass', because of its martial character and

* See L. Léger, *Histoire d'Autriche-Hongrie*, pp. 373 ff.

† We know that this was the Emperor's criticism of Mozart's opera.

the use of military instruments. Five analogous works
—the *Nelson Mass*, the *Theresa Mass*, and three ' solemn
masses '—bear the dates 1796, 1798, 1799, and 1801,
and consequently belong to the master's last period,
after the return from his second visit to England.

Haydn was not unaware that many of his hearers
were shocked by their lack of gravity. ' I cannot write
them otherwise ' he said. ' When I think of God, my
heart is so full of joy that the notes gush forth as from
a fountain. Since God gave me a joyful heart, he will
forgive me for having served him joyfully.'* It is
indeed true to say that ' at heart Haydn was as simple
as an artist of the Middle Ages '†, or at least that he
was a child of nature, for he had cast aside nothing of
his natural leanings or of the influences which shaped
his earliest mental development. At Rohrau, as in every
Christian village, the people connected the idea of
festival or rejoicing with that of the Sabbath rest and
of the Lord's day; the idea of divine beauty with that
of opulence: and just as the devotion of the crowd
clothed the ' miraculous image of the child Jesus ',
at Prag, with a robe of very stiff brocade and crowned
it with a diadem set with false jewels, so Haydn, on
the example of many Catholic musicians, would have
thought it impossible to be too prodigal, in a mass, of
all the pretentious adornments of his art. If we wish
to know what the masters of the eighteenth century,
under pressure of the tradition imposed by represen-
tatives of the *bel canto*, had made of the grave and
mysterious words in the Creed which declare the
doctrine of the Incarnation, and which the old contrapuntists loved to set in long-sustained passages
and solemn concatenations of chords, then we need
only consult Haydn's Mass *De Beata Virgine* in E
flat (1766):

* C. F. Pohl, *Joseph Haydn*, Vol. I, p. 357.
† Liliencron and Riehl in the *Allgemeine Deutsche Biographie*, art.
Haydn, Vol. XI, p. 142.

or his *Missa Cellensis* in C (1782):

Allowing his inspiration free play, as he has told us himself, he did not concern himself about any liturgical obligations. Each part of his masses begins with the words which, according to the canonical regulations, should be intoned by the priest, and which former masters refrained from setting to music. He does not scruple to isolate a word or a fragment of a line, which he repeats and brings in again while the other voices continue to follow the text*; or perhaps, if he finds

* In the *Mass for St. Cecilia* (1780) the word ' credo ' is sung as a refrain or interlude, in an ornate style, all through the Creed by the solo

that he has taken up too much time in developing the
early portions, he has no hesitation in distributing—
piling up, so to speak—bits of various phrases among
the different voices*. He uses choral fugues as adornments for the showy and brilliant choral sections which
alternate with ornate solos and the introductions or
symphonic flourishes. Thus his masses consist of very
mixed elements, and though their variety may help in
retaining the attention of an audience, it is, by its very
nature, fatal to the unity of composition, no less than
to its suitability for the purpose which is primarily
fixed by the sacred words.

One of the simplest of all Haydn's masses is that
for *St. John the Divine*, described as a ' little mass for
organ ' (1772), which has, in addition to the voices,
only two violin parts and a bass part for organ. The
longest is the *Mass for St. Cecilia*, in which the *Gloria*
is divided into seven parts. To pick out the most brilliant, we must choose between the *Nelson Mass* (1798)
and the *Drum Mass* (1790) in which a large orchestra
and animated rhythms confer a resemblance to a military pageant. The liveliest is probably the mass *De
Beata Virgine*, which concludes with this presto in six-
eight time† (See page 78).

The most popular, or, to be exact, the most frequently
performed in Germany in our own time, is the *Missa
Cellensis* or *Mariazeller-Messe*, composed in 1782, at
the request of an Austrian official for the monastery
of Mariazell in Styria, the same monastery to which
Haydn made a youthful pilgrimage many years before. In the *Benedictus* of this mass, he made use of an

soprano. In the *Mass for St. Nicolas* (also wrongly called *for St. Joseph*,
1772), it is the tenor who repeats four times the phrase 'et homo
factus est'.

* *Mass for St. Nicolas.*

† Perhaps this is the one to which Mendelssohn refers in his letter
from Düsseldorf, telling of his taking up the duties of organist, and
remarking ' Haydn's mass was scandalously merry '. (Mendelssohn,
Briefe, Vol. II. p. 10, letter dated 26th October 1833.)

air from his opera *Il Mondo della Luna*, composed some
years earlier. Similarly, in the *Missa Solemnis* in B flat
(1801), he introduced an air borrowed from his oratorio *The Creation*.

After the masses, the next in importance among
Haydn's Latin compositions is his *Stabat Mater* (1773)

for organ and orchestra, a long work divided into thirteen parts, the success of which helped considerably
to spread the fame of its writer. After its performances
in 1781, it was printed in Paris, then by Bland in
London. It was also translated into German, or rather
parodied, by Johann Adam Hiller, as a ' Passion ',
which has led certain writers to believe that Haydn
left an oratorio of this title. Considered as a great cantata for the concert hall, the *Stabat Mater* has many
interesting pages, some by reason of their melodic line,
some for their use of descriptive passages. We may say
of many parts, as of the *Salve Regina* for organ and
orchestra (1784) and of some of the motets, that, without being ' true religious music ', they are at least ' true
Haydn '.

The enormous number of motets attributed to him,
and the weakness of many of them, are explained and
excused up to a point by his careless compliance with
the solicitations of his admirers. Among other things,
it is said that his wife, incapable of appreciating his
works or even of taking pleasure in their success, but
very pious and very susceptible to flattery, made herself the stubborn advocate of the importunate priests
and monks who begged for a piece for their chapel.
And, as if this hasty productivity were not enough,
though often the only praiseworthy thing about it is
the flowing hand, industrious arrangers and counter-
feiters have done everything possible to spread abroad,
under cover of his name, pieces by other writers and
fragments borrowed from his instrumental works.

More than once, simply because of the similarity of
the name, and without any calculation or premedita-
tion, motets or symphonies by his brother, Michael
Haydn, were copied, sold, and performed, as works
by Joseph Haydn. This might not always have de-
tracted from his fame, for the distance between the
talents of the two brothers was less great than between
their fortunes. In religious composition, especially,

Michael sometimes excelled. He took a very different view of it from his brother's, although he also was a product of St. Stephen's, and consequently had come under the same influences at about the same age. These early impressions had however been effaced by others which came later, not from a master, or an habitual repertory, but from the profound and moving shocks of life. The loss of an only child whom the Salzburg organist never ceased to mourn, cast a shadow over his youth such as the *Kapellmeister* of Esterhaz had never known—a sorrow which we may blame or pity him for trying to drown, with his other cares, in wine. Of all the elements which go to form the ' religious sentiment', Joseph Haydn expressed only ' a boundless confidence in the mercy of God ' and, in his oratorios, ' admiration at the sight of the works of the Creator '. Michael Haydn, taught by tragic experience, learned to translate the idea of ' the weakness of man in presence of divine omnipotence '. That gravity which is strangely lacking in the Church music of the more illustrious brother is the very quality we praise in the Graduals of the younger.

One work, however, stands apart, by its gravity, in the series of religious compositions of the elder. Moreover, it has only a doubtful place there, for it can be classed equally well among his symphonies or his oratorios. It is a suite of seven sonatas, with an introduction and at the end a *terremoto* for orchestra, composed in 1785 on the ' Seven Words of our Redeemer on the Cross '*, at the request of a Spanish Canon, who wished to mingle some appropriate music with the meditations enjoined in the office of Holy Week, in order to heighten their effect. Having elbow

---

* The title of the first edition, published by Artaria in separate parts, was as follows: ' Musica instrumentale sopra le sette ultime parole del nostro Redentore in croce, o siano sette Sonate, con un introduzione, ed al fine un Teremoto, per due Violini, Viola, Violoncello, Flauto, Oboe, Corni, Clarini, Timpani, Fagotti e Contrabasso '.

room in the free form of the symphonic adagio, and being oriented only in a general direction by the series of sayings, which were declaimed in a bass recitative before each part, Haydn created one of his masterpieces.

Some years later, at Passau on his way to London, he heard an arrangement of the ' Seven Words ' for four voices and orchestra, set to German words, by Joseph von Friebert, *Kapellmeister* to the episcopal court of Passau. ' I think I could have done better ' said Haydn. Some time after his return, he took up his own score again, together with Friebert's version, and transformed his sonatas into so many accompanied choruses, adopting constantly the literary and musical work of his ' arranger ' in the first four parts. Between the fourth and fifth parts, he added a piece in sombre vein for wind instruments, thus dividing the whole composition into two suites. The work was published in its new form by Breitkopf at Leipzig in 1801*.

In spite of the attraction added by the choruses to the new version, it is in the first purely instrumental version that we can best study and most fully admire this beautiful work. One of the finest that Haydn has given us, its true character may be described by the single epithet ' elegiac '†.

ORATORIOS

Of all that Haydn heard in London, nothing surprised and interested him so much as the works of Handel. Not to mention mixed concerts, such as those of the ' Academy of Ancient Music ', in which a series of airs and detached pieces were given, he was present

* The history of this work and the comparison of Friebert's part with that of Haydn form the subject of an excellent study by A. Sandberger, which appeared in the *Jahrbuch der Musikbibliothek Peters für* 1903, pp. 47 ff.

† See Kretzschmar, *Führer durch den Concertsaal,* 2nd edition, Vol. II, Part I, p. 121.

on 23rd, 26th, and 28th May, and 1st June 1791, at
four meetings of the Handel Festival, at which a thousand vocalists and instrumentalists gave performances
of *Israel in Egypt*, the *Messiah*, the *Funeral Anthem*,
the *Coronation Anthem*, the *Jubilate*, and two complete
organ concertos, with extracts from *Saul*, *Judas Mac-
cabeus*, *Samson*, and *Jephtha*. The beauty of the works
and the magnificence of their interpretation made a
very strong impression on him. At the end of the
Hallelujah Chorus in the *Messiah*, he was heard to ex-
claim ' He is the greatest of us all! '* Thus, when the
idea of writing an oratorio was suggested to him by
Salomon during his second visit, he lent himself readily
to the realization of a proposal which would present
him as Handel's heir and successor, while the difference in their periods and temperaments prevented any
direct comparison between them.

Up to that time Haydn had only once attempted
the oratorio form†. In *Il Ritorno di Tobia* he conformed
to the customs of the Italo-Germanic school, fixed or
adopted by Hasse, Graun, Caldara, and Reutter, which
confused the forms of oratorio with those of opera‡.
The libretto of *The Creation*, founded on the book of
Genesis and Milton's *Paradise Lost*, was translated
from English into German by Gottfried van Swieten,
and remodelled to suit a taste which inclined all literature towards idyllic pictures of the harmonies of nature,
and which enabled Haydn to give to oratorio an

* In noting the effect produced on Haydn, Mozart, and Beethoven
by hearing or reading the works of Handel, we must bear in mind
that those of Johann Sebastian Bach were at the time almost unknown

† The oratorio *Abramo ed Isacco*, falsely attributed to Haydn, is now
known to have been written by Giuseppe Misliweczek.

‡ Reutter announced the secular or sacred character of his works by
the style of the overture. At the beginning of his operas he placed an
Italian overture, divided into three parts, at the beginning of his oratorios an overture in the French style, divided into two parts (introduction marked *grave* and a fugue marked *allegro*). Once this warning
was given, the rest of the score flowed into the usual mould.

entirely new interpretation, half religious and half
descriptive. Many a time already in his earlier works
he had taken a manifest pleasure in inserting into his
music more or less distinct musical pictures—tempests
at sea, in an air of *L'Incontro Improviso*, in the first scene
of *La Vera Costanza*, in a chorus added in 1784 to *Il
Ritorno di Tobia*, and in the work composed under the
title of *The Storm* for Salomon's concerts; an imitation
of the rhythm of the waves in a monologue in *Orlando
Paladino*; motifs suggesting sobs or ' torrents of tears '
in the *Stabat Mater*; noises of war or sounds of the
chase in various airs of the operas, overtures, and
symphonies. These scattered outlines were now to take
a firmer and preciser shape, and to acquire such proportions that the descriptive aspect of the poem and
the music becomes more important than its lyric and
sacred elements—hitherto regarded as the true source
and basis of biblical oratorio.

No doubt there are examples of descriptive music
to be found in Handel. In *Israel in Egypt* a multitude
of imitative passages illustrate the phases of an epic
story. But, as in portraits by primitive artists, the
human figure, in full relief, stands in the foreground,
and it is only through an open window, within the
perspective of a colonnade, or by the drawing aside of
a curtain, that we get a glimpse of a distant landscape
of singular depth and detail. Haydn's method is exactly
the opposite. The landscape is the central feature of
his picture, and man is surrounded by exaggerated
details, and deep shadows, which, having their own
beauty apart from him, sometimes, to his detriment,
usurp the principal place.

The Creation opens with a representation of chaos.
We need not ask whether a Berlioz, twenty-five years
later, or even a Lesueur in Haydn's own time, would
have found material in such a subject for more striking
developments, made up of bolder motifs, harsher dis-
sonances, and more crashing sonorities. In spite of, or

perhaps, because of the splendours of expression to which the masters of modern orchestral music have accustomed us, we must admire the simplicity of the means by which ' papa Haydn ', with skill and not without grandeur, has achieved so difficult a task. For Haydn, who ' thought in sonatas ' and for whom all musical ideas were born crystallized in symmetrical shape, chaos consisted in the negation of order and traditional regularity. It is certainly in this way that he tries to create impression of it in his hearers. Instead of the rounded phrases and balanced periods which usually express his argument in clear terms, the logical development of which the mind and ear of the listener may afterwards take pleasure in following, he uses phrases which seem to be cut off and incomplete, by means of which he desires to arouse a feeling of suspense and uncertainty. The heavier the weight of the suspense, the more miraculous will be the effect of the chord of C major, suddenly struck by all the voices and instruments together, on the words ' And there was light '*.

The whole series of recitatives and airs by which the three archangels announce and explain the phases of the creation, is treated in the same descriptive manner, with a continual regard for image-building detail. God having separated day from night, confusion ceases and order reigns: a short modulating passage, con-

* Mme. de Staël, who had heard *The Creation* in Vienna, said of this famous passage and the descriptive pieces following it, that Haydn ' used his wit to the abuse of his talent ', and she quoted sympathetically the remark of a hearer, to the effect that one had to stop up one's ears when the light gushed forth. (*De l'Allemagne*, chap. xxxii.) In the same passage a curious example occurs of the alterations which found their way into his clearest works through false interpretations becoming traditional. In 1872 W. Oppel, in the *Allgemeine Musikalische Zeitung* (No. 30, 24th July 1872), told how a choral society of Leipzig had long been accustomed to lead up by a crescendo to the last word in the phrase, ' And there was light ', and how a new conductor, going by the sense of the words and the directions on the score, only succeeded with difficulty and after long discussion in changing this unfortunate gradation.

cise and agitated, gives place to peaceful, diatonic
music, with the key clearly defined. The spirits of darkness sink into eternal night: the direction of the motif
indicates their fall, and the choir completes the picture
of confusion by building up canonical responses on
this motif. Then, as soon as the infernal host has disappeared, the chorus, in a clear and joyous melody,
sings of the new world which has arisen at the divine
command. The ingenious beauty of these oppositions
would lead us to accept them as the inspirations of
genius, if Haydn, in working them out, had been
able to free himself from the tyrannical laws of form.
The *da capo*, the tedious *da capo* of Italian opera, by
repeating an effect the whole virtue of which lies in its
realism, destroys this virtue and reduces the effect to
that of a mere artifice. Must we then confess that
Haydn's music, like his face in the portraits painted
over a period of forty years, remains unchangingly
surmounted by the wig he would never give up? And,
everything considered, are we to reproach him with
it? Is it not heedlessly that we dare to smile? The
moulds of Haydn's thought are suitable to its content.
To break with them would have been a revolutionary
action on his part, and would have entailed the risk of
incongruities which would shock us more than a few
wrinkles on a forehead. We love the works of Haydn
for their sincerity, their honesty, even for their calm
ingenuousness, no less than for their healthy and cheerful vigour, and their constant serenity. Let us not
bring too many of the refinements of modern criticism
into our examination of *The Creation*. Let us rejoice
with Haydn in the beauty of the world:

Let us tarry with him to see the rivers rolling their
even waves in rhythmic flow, and the hills rising in
leaps of fifths and sixths. Let us listen to the streams
murmuring in the meadows and the angel Gabriel
singing, in ornate style and pastoral rhythm, the per-
fumed breath of the flowers:

Let us follow, one by one, the miracles of the divine
week, and let us join, as in a temple, in the pious senti-
ments which the choir, drawing its inspiration from
the Psalms of David, expresses in magnificent counterpoint. The first part closes with the words ' The heavens
are telling the glory of God '. In the second part, after
Gabriel has evoked the pleasant twittering of the birds,
and Raphael—a bass—the sporting of the fishes in
the depths of the waters, after we have heard the lion
roar on a trill on D flat, the tiger spring, and the stag,
and the horse, on rhythms appropriate to their various
motions, when even the insects have passed by—as in
a picture by Breughel or a Noah's ark made in Nürn-
berg—the trio of archangels interrupts the description
of this animated scene with a fervent lyric hymn, ' How
many are Thy works, O God ' (See page 87). ' The
Lord is great ' replies the chorus, and above its
powerful harmonies the voices of the soloists rise in
exultant fiorituri.

The fine *Alleluia*, developed as a double fugue,
closes the second part, and marks the climax of the
work. In spite of all the beauties scattered through the
remainder of the score, a feeling of lassitude gradually
gains upon the hearer, owing to the great length, but

partly also to the unreasonable desire, which one cannot resist, to see Haydn rise to still greater heights,
and surpass himself yet again, when, after the descriptive passages are over, the action begins; that is,
when the narrative of the three archangels is completed
by the story of the creation of man and woman, and
these latter begin to take part. The melodies which fall
to their share are no less flowing, no less favourable to
the voice, and no less agreeable to the ear, than those
given over to the interpretation of the former soloists.
In their first duet, Haydn invented a kind of chanted

accompaniment, which was quite new and which many
musicians have imitated:

The chorus that links together this duet, brilliant
in accompaniment, and the final chorus, compounded
with vigorous *tutti* and florid fugal quartets, are no
less admirable in composition, no less powerful in
effect, than the first and second parts. Their only fault
is that they prolong the eloquence without sufficiently
renewing it.

An anecdote will show to what extent Haydn be-
lieved he was composing a purely religious work in
writing *The Creation.*

A cleric named Ockl, vicar of the parish of St. John,
near Plan, in Bohemia, and a great admirer of Haydn,
resolved in 1801 to organize a performance of *The
Creation* in his church. While making active prepara-
tions, he thought it his duty to ask permission from

the Consistory at Prag—a permission which, to his great astonishment, was refused, and with which his flock, tempted by the prospect of a musical treat, proposed to dispense. To safeguard the vicar from all responsibility, they sent him for a drive some distance away while the concert took place. However, a few days later, vehement criticisms were launched from the pulpit in a neighbouring village, against an entertainment which ' only heathens could have allowed to take place in a sacred building '. Much troubled by this public disapproval, the poor vicar wrote two letters to Haydn asking him the true meaning of the work. The reply he received must have reassured him at least upon the purity of the musician's intentions. Haydn affirmed that ' no church could be profaned by *The Creation* ', but rather that his music would influence its hearers to pray to- and honour the Creator much better than preaching of the kind that had been reported to him. In great indignation, the old master characterized the affair as ' very ridiculous ', and announced his intention, in case the Consistory would not reverse its veto, of carrying the matter himself before ' Their Majesties who have never heard the oratorio unmoved, and who are convinced of the value of this sacred work '*.

The Seasons, which Haydn composed immediately after *The Creation*, could not pretend to this distinction of a ' sacred work ', and was only connected by external bonds with the oratorio form, by its proportions and its suitability for the concert hall. It is a series of *genre* pictures, ' a garland of cantatas ', of a descriptive nature, with a ' moral ' spoken from time to time, as in the classic fables, most fittingly by the voice of serene old age.

The instrumental introduction to *The Seasons*, like

* Haydn's letter was reproduced by the *Allgemeine Musikalische Zeitung*, Leipzig, 21st January 1874, according to other German periodicals.

that of *The Creation*, has a literary programme. It is
intended to depict the passage from winter to spring,
and is connected by a few short responses in recitative
form with the chorus of peasants saluting the season
of beauty. Beethoven in his *Pastoral Symphony*

had in mind one of the rustic melodies of this first
chorus:

A surprising freshness, abundance, and liveliness
of impression, such as one would normally expect
from youth, fill the whole work. The light canvas provided by the poet seems to invite the old master to
revive all the memories of his long and peaceful life.
Haydn recalls the beauty of spring in the country
where he was born, and in the midst of which he lived,
the labourer whistling a merry tune as he leans his
arms on the handles of the plough, the sower whose
rhythmic gestures scatter the seed in the furrows, and
whom the little ' Sepperl ' once followed round about
Rohrau in the pleasant morning mist. He uses a theme
from one of his London symphonies in the accompaniment to one of their songs, as though he still wishes
to associate himself with their labours. Long ago,
among the herbage on the banks of the Leitha or the
Neusiedler See, he saw the first light of dawn, the
flight of birds at night, the scattering of the flocks; he
saw the crests of the hills grow red in the summer sun,
whose splendour he celebrates in a beautiful trio with
chorus. Round about Esterhaz, he used to hunt the

partridge, the hare, and the deer. It is himself he pictures in the hunting song, delightful in its melodious candour, with an animated and persistent accompaniment suggesting the guest of the dogs. It is the whole equipage of Prince Esterhazy which gallops, shouts, and sings in the chorus ' Hört das laute Getön! ' The festival of the vintage is no less full of life and movement, and is as unsophisticated in character as the little love duet of Lucas and Hännchen, and the songs of the spinners and of the peasants assembled in the winter evening.

The master everywhere delights in descriptive detail, but he does not forget that music can have a loftier mission. In connection with the harvest, he writes an almost religious eulogy of work, ' O Fleiss, O edler Fleiss, von dir kommt alles Heil ', beautiful and solemn words from a man, who, exalting labour in song, had set an example of it all his life up to his old age. Haydn prays too. The sight of the finished world strengthens his faith and gratitude. His labourer's song has for complement a prayer for the fruits of the earth. His picture of Spring concludes solemnly in a kind of *Laudate*. And at the end of the work, after he has enumerated with cheerful heart a few of the reasons man has for loving life, he refuses to interpret winter as a symbol of death. The ascent of the righteous to the gates of heaven symbolizes the eternal re-birth which rises out of the apparent destruction. The liturgical *Amen*, prolonged by all the voices on the final chord, has all the significance of the *Et vitam venturi saeculi* which concludes the Creed in the Catholic liturgy.

Thus Haydn's oratorios correct the error into which an examination of his religious music might lead us. His masses, which offend our taste by the appearance of a light and worldly style, are not the work of an unbeliever. They emanate from a simple and childlike optimism, which the oratorios develop and state in its

completeness. In *The Creation*, Haydn had rendered
the verses from Genesis which tell how God, having
looked upon His work, saw that it was good, and on
that he had based his whole philosophy.* This, in a
flash, illumines all his art. Joy, the end of music as of
life, leaves no room for indifference or bitterness. The
calm of soul to which it gives rise and which it main-
tains through the conflict of passions and the outward
events of life, corresponds in artistic language with
regularity of form, which, far from confining thought
within the burdensome and rigid limits, lends itself
with suppleness to its movements, and allows them to
set their own harmonious bounds. Since Goethe's
saying, ' The classic is the hale man, the romantic the
sick man ', has been so many times repeated, let us
apply it to Haydn, for, at least in the world of music,
we shall never find a more excellent example to con-
firm it.

INSTRUMENTAL MUSIC

Haydn is in his element with instrumental music.
There, freed from the constraint of words, he can give
rein to the abundance of his thought, which he himself
once compared, speaking of his religious music, to the
gush of water that escapes from an overflowing fountain. Certainly the living stream, wearing a bed for
itself, rippling and leaping through woods and among
mossy stones, giving drink to the squirrels and the
birds, and playing hide-and-seek with the sunshine
under the shadow of the ferns, is not more fresh and
restful to the traveller coming from the heights than
is the music of Haydn to the musician long habituated
to the towering peaks of ancient and modern art. The
smallness of the frame, astonishing at first, and at

* See *Allgemeine Deutsche Biographie*, art. *Haydn*, by Liliencron
and Riehl.

which some are inclined to smile, envelops the minutest
details in an atmosphere of intimacy in which the charm
of very simple language is felt. One submits to [it
willingly, and it is only later, when the time comes for
analysis and reflection, that one discovers how wrong
was the first impression of a careless, childish, spon-
taneous art. Haydn sings ingenuously, from the depths
of his heart: he composes scientifically with all his intelligence.

If we try to take to pieces the machinery of his instrumental compositions, we find it very simple, and
though in the course of time, profiting by the experience
of others, he was able to make it work more skilfully
and surely, its modifications are not so profound as to
baffle our understanding. Rarely do we find such per-
fact unity, such peaceful progress, in the development
of an artistic career. Instead of requiring classification
and division into distinct periods or opposing types,
Haydn's instrumental production may be regarded as
a whole, for which we could, if need be, give a general
definition almost without regard to the chronology of
its component parts.

If we are to believe Michael Kelly, the author of
The Creation placed melodic invention above all else.
The position the Irish singer attributes to him in
his *Reminiscences* is of great interest in the study of
his style. ' It is the air ' said Haydn ' which constitutes
the charm of music, and it is the air which is the most
difficult thing to produce. Patience and study enable
one to put together agreeable sounds, but the invention of a beautiful melody is an act of genius. The truth
is that a beautiful melody can give pleasure without
either adornment or accompaniment. To find out
whether it is really beautiful, it should be sung without
accompaniment.'

The constitution of the melody, in Haydn's case,
has therefore rightly held the attention of musical
experts; and if certain theories, to which this research

has given rise, have gone rather beyond their aim, it is because other interests capable of destroying the impartiality of the inquiry have been mingled with the motives of pure learning. The particularist or separatist form of local patriotism, which still flourishes in the Succession States of the Austro-Hungarian Empire, has attempted to claim Haydn as a representative of the Slav races, and has boldly declared him a Croatian composer. The basis of this theory was provided by Dr. Kuhač, a student of folk-lore, in the comparison which he attempts between a number of themes or fragments of themes by Haydn, drawn chiefly from the best-known works of his maturity, and an equal number of scraps of melody from popular ballads, songs, and dance tunes, collected from oral tradition in districts of Lower Austria, where ethnological elements of Slav origin are more or less plainly distinguishable. The thematic analogies pointed out by Dr. Kuhač seem to him to indicate direct borrowings by Haydn from the national repertory of Croatian fiddlers and singers, and he interprets them as the visible sign of a Slav descent*. To explain why these resemblances exist only in the later works, he conjectures that the influences of his youth and his sojourn in Vienna as a young man must have temporarily effaced in him these native recollections which were revived much later, on the shores of the Neusiedler See, by the neighbourhood of populations of the same stock.

Dr. Kuhač's thesis has been adopted with enthusiasm by an English musical authority, Sir W. H. Hadow, who has been its principal supporter†. Before

* Haydn would be a descendant of Slav immigrants settled near Rohrau one hundred and fifty or two hundred years before his birth; his name would be an alteration of the usual form Hajden, and his mother's name would be written Kolar instead of Koller. In support of these suppositions, a signature of the master is adduced in which he happened to insert an e, Giuseppe Hayden.

† Sir W. H. Hadow accepts it as proved, and adopts it unreservedly in his little volume Haydn, a Croatian Composer, in his

subscribing to it, we should like to have before our eyes some documents of an earlier date, or at least some indications prior to Haydn's own epoch. For why should not the terms of the proposition be reversed? During the time he lived at Eisenstadt or Esterhaz, when his music resounded day and night in the castle and gardens of his prince, why should not his own airs, or scraps at least of his own melodies, have stolen through the open windows, and remained in the memories, first of the people whose duty it was to interpret them, or who were obliged to hear them, and then of the scattered population of the surrounding country? The mishaps of too confident folk-lorists, who have allowed airs and songs quite definitely reaching the villages from the suburbs and the theatres, to stray into their collections of so-called folk-music, should make us excessively prudent. What is sometimes mistaken for a wild shrub is a sucker thrown off from the spreading roots of a great tree, which extends its invisible network far and wide under the ground.

The curious spirit of investigation and lively emulation which drove contrapuntists of the old school to work on a given theme, or to borrow popular or artistic themes openly from one another, and to make parade of all their knowledge, all their subtlety, in treating them differently, had disappeared from musical custom. When Haydn chose the form of ' variations ' for the andantes of his sonatas, quartets, and symphonies, he provided the necessary theme himself.

Only occasionally some special intention seems to have led him to choose a starting point elsewhere. C. F. Pohl has clearly shown that the famous ' romance ' volume (*The Viennese Period*) of the Oxford History of Music, of which he is the editor, and also in his revision of the article on Haydn for the new edition of Grove's *Dictionary of Music and Musicians*. H. Conrat, of London, supports the same view in an article in *Die Musik* in 1905. The full titles of all these publications will be found in the bibliography at the end of this volume. See also an article by W. Ritter, in *S.I.M.*, 1910, No. 1.

of one of his Parisian symphonies—the one called
La reine de France—is based on a French arietta, *La
gentille et jeune Lisette.* May we assume some connection between the adoption of this melody and the title
given by Haydn or his publishers to this symphony ?
Was this a favourite ' romance ' of the sovereign he
had known as Archduchess? The origin of the little
French piece is obscure. Evidently its simplicity
pleased Haydn for he used it again, or thought of it,
in writing a concerto for the *lira,* and yet again later in
the allegretto of one of his London symphonies—the
so-called *Military Symphony.* It was rare for him to
return in this way to earlier ideas*. A resemblance,
limited to a few brief thematic fragments in the andante
of his symphony *La Poule,* might suggest a passing
allusion to Rameau's celebrated piece for the harpsichord, which bears the same title:

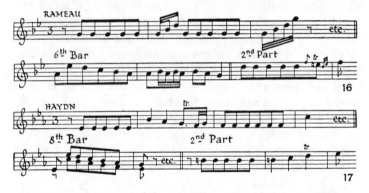

A bulky pamphlet was published in 1845, by Anton
Schmid, to refute the assertion of a journalist, according to which Haydn had used an air by Zingarelli in
composing his Austrian Hymn. This polemic had long
been forgotten when Dr. Kuhač came along and placed

* The principal theme of his symphony, *Roxelane,* is to be found in
the overture to *Il mondo della Luna.* The finale of the symphony, *The
Hunt,* is the old overture of *La Fedelta Premiata.* A motif from *The
Creation* gives its name to the mass in which it is used.

the same piece among those of which Haydn had borrowed the elements from popular Croatian song. In a mocking tone which, however, covered a serious argument, Wilhelm Tappert showed that precisely those parts of the motif claimed as Slav figured in a rondo for the harpsichord by Telemann, printed in 1728 at Hamburg, and that if one pushed the matter further back, step by step, its origin was finally discovered in the intonation of the Lord's Prayer in the Catholic liturgy, which had also inspired the popular Alsatian song *O Strassburg*, the song *O wie wohl ist mir am Abend*, and the chant *Dir dank' ich heute*. Another fragment bears a similar resemblance to an anonymous dance tune, printed in 1788 at Leipzig, in a collection called *Terpsichore*. ' If then ' says Wilhelm Tappert ' the Austrian Hymn consists of a total of fifty-six notes, and of these thirteen belong to the Croatian song, and seventeen to a dance by an unknown author, what is left for Haydn? There remains as his own, in spite of everything, the whole Austrian Hymn ' *—since he alone was able to create, or re-create, from all the fragments of diverse material a living and beautiful work.

As regards Haydn's melodic origins, all analogies, intentions, or reminiscences noticeable in his music are mere coincidences which can lead to no certain result. If some few motifs seem to place him as a Croat, and if the exuberance, gaiety, and freedom of his minuets would persuade us to class him as a true Viennese, the broad and sustained themes in the slow movements of his works, appearing always under rich ornamentation, have led to his classification as an *Italian*, an epithet intended as blame or praise, according to the mode of the moment.

* W. Tappert, *Die Österreichische Nationalhymne*, in *Die Musik*, June 1905. Haydn's melody has been adapted in Germany to the words *Deutschland über alles*, and in America to those of a Protestant hymn, ' Glorious things of Thee are spoken '.

The truth is that Haydn's melodies, like all the
expressions of human thought, are compounded of
many parts, influenced by continual exchanges, closely
related to those of a great number of musicians, important and unimportant, living at the same period,
submitted in fact to the hidden laws which govern each
age in the history of art, laws incessantly revised, and
disobeyed only by a few rare creative intelligences,
who dictate others in their place.

To estimate with fairness the part played by popular
echoes in Haydn's work, we must take into account
all that music of the tavern and the open air in the
midst of which he lived at Vienna for so many years
of his youth, songs of the street, drinking songs, sub-
urban dance tunes, scraps from the works of the masters,
played at the cross-roads or in the back regions of shops
by bands of poor devils, whose occupation, like his
own, was to play or copy music for the amusement of
tipplers or of passers-by. This was his first public: he
served its habits and formed himself upon its taste,
before entering the service of a prince who demanded,
above all, productivity.

As Karl Krebs has pointed out, the means are lacking
for an intimate study of the methods of composition
of Haydn and Mozart, which we are enabled to make
in the case of Beethoven, thanks to his note-books.
They do not seem to have needed long periods of
meditation for the production of *Don Giovanni* and the
symphonies. ' With Mozart, composition was almost
invariably in the nature of improvisation; with Haydn,
it was ordered and methodical work.' Laborious work it
was too, to judge by some manuscripts, notably that of
the *Austrian Hymn*, one of the relics of the master in the
Imperial Library at Vienna, in which we see that, far
from being written in a single uprush, the melody is
the result of patient study.

It is because he held the ' motif ' to be supreme
among the materials of composition that we always find

him giving so clear, so distinct, so definite, and so constantly regular a form to the first outlines of his musical thought. His melody is made up of symmetrical sections, linked one to another, with repeats, interruptions, and foreordained periods. Here the relationship is plain between his instrumental music and that of the preceding century. He no longer uses the old forms of dance tunes, except only the minuet, which is the most modern, and the most characteristically Viennese: but he is haunted by the memory of the traditional rhythms, with fixed breaks and repetitions, imposed on the musician by the movements of the dancers. His motifs seem to adapt themselves to a regular pattern, which cuts up the page into groups of four or eight bars. Such are the light, familiar, almost variety-hall themes, of the Symphony in D (No. 86 in the complete works; No. 129 in Wotquenne's catalogue):

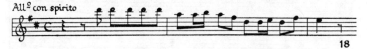

of the London symphonies, numbers 5, 7, and 8, and of the symphony *Les Adieux*, which concludes in so unexpected and original a manner, because of its programme. It opens on a theme analagous to the *bourrée:*

and, in the same style, that of the great quartet in B flat of opus 76, in which the pretty contrapuntal setting of the motif conceals the monotony of its repetitions: (See page 100.)

The ornaments indicated by Haydn formed an integral part of his melodic designs, and he greatly disliked the addition of others—a temptation which his

20

interpreters probably found it very difficult to resist
when all the traditions of the age incited them to it.
Twenty-five years after Haydn's death, the violinist,
Ferdinand David, had not yet got rid of the habit,
handed down to him by older *virtuosi*, of adding variations or improvised elaborations in the recapitulation

of the allegro, when taking the part of first violin in
Haydn's quartets. The cheerful jollity of the motifs,
their clearness, and the equilibrium preserved in their
distribution among the participating instruments, could
not but be disturbed and destroyed under additional
burdens out of all proportion to their power of resis-
tance. The master of Esterhaz, not a very skilful performer on any instrument, though he played several,
allowed to his interpreters a considerable virtuosity in
his adagios, variations, and rondos; his well-balanced
imagination ventured as far as the capriccio; but all the
touches and embellishments remain characteristically
melodious, cheerful, and regular.

A feeling for tonality was no less important a part of
his inspiration than that of rhythmic symmetry. He
was attracted by clear tones, the major mode. He liked
to state, or rather proclaim the chosen key in the
opening bar, by striking the common chord, or by
picking out its notes one by one in either rising or
descending order. At the beginning of a piece, he
frequently places an accidental or a *gruppetto*, which
performs the function, more tonal than rhythmic, of
accentuating the essential keynote. The anxiety and
uneasiness which are born from an uncertain or modulating opening passage, and which lend to its ' resolution ' so much power and so much attraction to the ear,
are *terra incognita* to the musicians of this period. Peaceful and conservative people, they lived securely under
the absolute dominion of the tempered scale, and
whether from a desire to conform with custom, or in
consequence of the feverish taste with which they were
all obliged to work, they drew largely upon the great
stock of formulas and commonplaces which each
generation turns again for its own use. It is these commonplaces or musical idioms, which Haydn helps to establish or which he simply accepts, that constitute the true
resemblance between his melodic, rhythmic, and har-
monic types and those of his contemporaries. Many

motifs could be drawn from their works that would
appear interchangeable: but their comparison with
Haydn ceases—a very true observation made by Karl
Krebs—as soon as it becomes a question of the use of
this material or the art of development, in which the
master of Rohrau had almost no rival, except Mozart.

*
* *

Even in Haydn's own lifetime people were already
inquiring what his models had been. ' I have found
the source of Haydn's style ' cried Misliweczek, on
hearing a symphony by Giovanni Battista Sammartini.
The remark, repeated to Haydn, annoyed him, and he
described as a scribbler the Milanese musician who
had suddenly been pointed out as his model. He declared that he had been influenced by nothing but
the sonatas of Carl Philipp Emmanuel Bach. But
modern historians, to whom this single reference
seemed rightly inadequate, have succeeded in adducing
other names from the vast accumulation of forgotten
work of the same period. Quite a little army of artists
finds a place in the genealogical table of the origin of
the great instrumental forms, in which Haydn no longer
plays the part, so long attributed to him, of miraculous
inventor. There was scarcely any attempt, because of
the small difference in age, to count Gossec as his forerunner.* There was scarcely any hesitation in admitting
that the symphony—the supreme form of pure music
—was the product of a sudden act of genius, like a
meteor fallen from the sky. In the domain of musical
composition, as in that of the other arts and sciences,
such power has never belonged to an individual man.
Haydn's glory will not be lessened when, as a result
of successful research, the foundations are discovered
upon which he raised such lasting monuments.

* We held this opinion twenty-five years ago, though the state of
historical research at that period did not allow of its establishment.

The *Suite*, in the hands of the seventeenth-century masters, was a series of pieces arranged almost immutably in the same order—an overture and several dances—connected by the conformity of key, and sometimes by the repetition of the same theme with rhythmical and other modifications. Then came the innovation, to which we cannot give a definite date, by which the overture became detached from the *Suite* and appeared as an independent work, itself divided into three movements. Sandberger has unearthed the title of a book of separate overtures by Schiefferdecker from a catalogue dated 1748, and from that of Breitkopf for 1765, the advertisement of more than a hundred similar works, French overtures or *intrades*, by Fasch, Förster, Graun, Hasse, Hertwig, Pfeiffer, Telemann, and other Germans of the North or South. Most of these pieces date from a period much earlier than that of the catalogue, for already in 1740, the critics were censuring the overture and finding it antiquated and old-fashioned. This reproach, it is thought, referred to the middle part of the composition, treated as a *fugato*, the scholastic style of which was beginning to weary the public. The more modern musicians, however, were turning towards the light and attractive allegros of the Italian overture. The first half of the eighteenth century saw an unprecedented increase in the number of instrumental works, and a similar growth in the confusion of the terms by which they were described. The *Divertissements*, *Cassations*, *Quadri*, *Serenades*, and *Nocturnes*, had no fixed rules to control the plan or the number of pieces; and there was no clear understanding on the meaning of *Chamber* Sonata and *Church* Sonata. The forms, like the terminology, remained vague and fluctuating.

In the midst of this period of transition and elaboration, the success of the sonata in three parts, of the type of Emmanuel Bach's and of the first symphonies, in three or four parts, was perhaps due to the fact that their plan contained certain fixed elements, thus giving a restful impression of order.

The constitution of the modern orchestra is so closely linked to the organization of the symphonic form that it is impossible to tell which of these two great historical facts was the cause, and which the effect, of the other. Similarly, among the great number of musicians concerned, it is impossible to arrange in true succession the names of those who definitely led the way.

Johann Stamitz, founder of the Mannheim school, is now recognized to have been, if not absolutely Haydn's forerunner, at least considerably earlier in date. Born at Deutschbrod in Bohemia, on 19th June 1717, discovered and engaged at Frankfurt, in 1742, by Prince Karl Theodor, who became Elector Palatine the following year, Stamitz lived at Mannheim from 1745 to the time of his death in 1757 or 1758. Burney, who passed through the town some fifteen years later, found his memory still green, and did not hesitate to attribute positively to him the invention of the symphony, saying that ' stimulated by the productions of Jommelli, he had for the first time extended the limits of the ordinary operatic overture, which was only used in the theatre'. Without taking the words of the English traveller too literally, it is obvious that in 1772, when Haydn's fame was firmly established, Stamitz was generally recognized to be his forerunner. He was, in fact, one of the first to cultivate and popularize the symphony. His journey to Paris in 1754 gives us precise indications of this. During his stay of about a year in France, Stamitz appeared as composer and as performer on the violin and the *viola d'amore* at the private concerts of the financier, La Pouplinière, and at the meetings of the *Concert Spirituel* and the *Concert Italien*. At the *Concert Spirituel* he gave a new symphony for horns and oboes on 8th September 1754, and a symphony with clarinets and horns on 26th March 1755. A few months later, his famous book was printed and on sale in Paris, containing *Six sonates à trois parties concertantes qui sont faites pour exécuter ou à trois ou avec tout orchestre**, which we now call by the abbreviated title of ' trios for orchestra ', and look upon as one of the first monuments of the symphonic art. It belongs in fact to the modern style of instrumental music, by its suppression of the continuo and by the plan and division of the parts.

Before the arrival of Stamitz, the Parisian public was already accustomed to hear in concerts orchestral works entitled symphonies, not all of which are known to us, which sprang from the type of the *overture* divided into three movements, or of the *sonata*. The programmes of the *Concert Spirituel* from 1750 onwards, advertised *symphonies* by Plessis, Desormeaux, J. B. Chrétien, Pla, and Filippo Palma—by the last-named a symphony with horns, performed on 15th August 1752. In 1753 a sonata by Mondonville had been set for full orchestra. In the course of the same year the music sellers advertized two sets of ' six symphonies for three violins and bass ', one by Labbé (the son) and the other by the younger Caraffe, a collection of *Sei Sinfonie de differenti autori*, published by the horn-player Ebert, and a book of six symphonies by Moyreau. Some of these works, like the symphonies of Papavoine, published in 1752, remain in subjection to the old traditions in their use of the continuo. Others are independent of it. At the same time as Stamitz, another musician, Giuseppe Touchemolin, also from Germany, first violin to the Elector of Saxony, had a 'symphony for horns ' performed at the *Concert Spirituel* on 15th August 1754; and in the month of August 1755, the publisher, Venier, began to issue his collections of

---

* This work, sold in Paris by the author in the rue Saint-Jacques, and by Mlle. Vandome, M. Louvet, and M. Bayard, appeared on 12th August 1755, under licence granted to ' Johann Stamitz, director of instrumental music and *Kapellmeister* to His Serene Highness the Elector Palatine'.

symphonies *de varii autori*, which ultimately reached
the number of fourteen, while some of his competitors
hastened to place on sale works of a similar kind in
considerable numbers. These facts, which have hitherto not been sufficiently stressed, are important, at least
as regards the distribution of the first symphonies: for
this activity on the part of the French publishers was
promptly echoed in Holland and England. It is from
copies engraved or printed in Paris that we know to-
day the greater number of the instrumental works of
the Mannheim School. It was in Paris that a symphony
by Haydn was printed for the first time*. And it is
through a French edition that Richter's rights are
confirmed, for the licence granted to Dutés to publish
in two volumes ' twelve symphonies by Mr. Richter '
is dated 22nd February 1744, and therefore precedes
by twelve years the appearance of Stamitz's orchestral
trios†.

Franz Xaver Richter, born on 1st December 1709, at
Höllischau in Moravia, held the post of assistant
Kapellmeister to the Prince-Abbot of Kempten in Suabia
from 1740. Thence he went to Mannheim in 1748,
and to Strassburg in 1769. The symphonies published
in Paris, in 1744, therefore preceded his arrival in
Mannheim. The traces of stiffness which Dr. Hugo
Riemann finds in them are explained by their relative
antiquity, compared with those of Stamitz and his
immediate disciples or rivals in Mannheim—Joseph

---

* In 1764 the publisher Venier included a quartet by Haydn, under
the title of ' symphony ', in his fourteenth collection of symphonies *de
varii autori*, which was advertised as ' Unknown authors worth knowing ' in the *Avant-Coureur* of 26th March 1764. It contained six compositions by Van Malder, Heyden, Bach, Pfeiffer, Hehetky (Schetky),
and Frantzl. It is therefore incorrect to say that the first symphony of
Haydn's known in France was introduced by Sieber or Fonteski in
1770.

† See the author's study, *La Librairie musicale en France de* 1653 *à*
1790 in the *Recueil trimestriel de la Société internationale de musique*,
8th year, 1906-7, p. 443.

Toeschi, Anton Filtz, Ignaz Holzbauer, and Christian
Cannabich. All these composers were very prolific. Dr.
Riemann has catalogued forty-five symphonies and
ten trios for orchestra by Johann Stamitz, sixty-two
symphonies by Richter, thirty-nine by Filtz, sixty-five
by Holzbauer, sixty-two by J. Toeschi, and ninety-
one by Cannabich.* At the same time many other
musicians were working on the same subject with
equal zeal. Willibald Nagel has counted one hundred
and eighteen symphonies by Carl Graupner, who
died in 1760 at Darmstadt. J. F. Fasch (1688-1759),
who served the Prince of Anhalt-Zerbst, Chr. Förster
(1693-1745), who was attached to the staff of the
Prince of Schwarzburg-Rudolstadt, the brothers Graun
(Heinrich, 1701-1759, and Johann Gottlob, 1698-
1771), who lived in Berlin, and Leopold Mozart
(1719-1787), were all of them seniors and predecessors
of Haydn.

In 1745 the symphony was a type sufficiently well-
known in Northern Germany for Scheibe to speak of it
with praise in his *Kritischer Musicus*. He described it as
a composition divided into three movements, of which
the first was modelled on a plan in two parts, while the
second was a modified repetition of the first, with
modulations and the addition of ' unexpected inventions '. The introduction of the minuet as the fourth
movement of a symphony is considered to be an innovation due to the Mannheim group. Nagel finds it
in forty-eight of the one hundred and eighteen symphonies of Graupner ; Leopold Mozart used it at an
early date ; and a double minuet serves as finale to the
first of the six short symphonies of Papavoine.

It would be very difficult to guess which of all these
compositions came under the notice of Haydn, either
when he was living in Vienna and playing in the little

* See Dr. Riemann's preface and the list at the beginning of Vol. I
of the symphonies of the Bavarian Palatinate School, published in the
collection of the *Denkmäler deutscher Tonkunst*, 3rd year, Part I.

orchestras, or when he went there daily to play, conduct, and compose orchestral music for his first patrons,
Fürnberg and von Morzin. It is most improbable
that he could be ignorant of the work of the Viennese
composers, J. G. Reutter, his former master at St.
Stephen's, Georg Matthias Monn (1717-1750),
Matthäus Schlöger (1722-1766), Georg Christoph
Wagenseil (1715-1777), and Joseph Starzer (1727-
1787). Some of the works of these musicians have
recently been published* and contrasted with those of
the Mannheim group. They are especially interesting
because of the relation they undoubtedly bear to the
early inspirations of Haydn. When he went, as a poor
choir-boy, to earn a few pence by helping with the
plates and dishes in the house of some great lord, he
heard similar works to Reutter's suite, *Servizio di
tavola*, which comprises a noisy initial allegro, a larghetto, a minuet with trio, and a finale. And when he
played the violin in the serenading orchestras, he may
have played or heard Monn's symphonies, including
the one in D, dated 1740, in which the allegro with its
two themes, its rather sketchy development section,
and its recapitulation, contains, in a sort, the promise
of the future symphonic first-movement form. The
same piece includes also an aria, a minuet without trio,
and a finale in a popular, or one might say ' Haydn-
esque' style. Similarly, Wagenseil, in a symphony dated
1746, and in another one undated, sketches out a
double motif in the allegro, and uses the minuet, in
the first case as finale, in the second as third movement,
with a frolicsome finale.

What gives these little works an old-fashioned air
is the retention of the *cembalo* with the thorough-bass,
with which the symphonic orchestra was soon to dispense. Such, however, is the power of long tradition,

* *Denkmäler der Tonkunst in Osterreich*, Vol. XV, Part 2, 1908,
Symphonies of the Viennese School, published by Karl Horwitz and
Karl Riedel, with a preface by Dr. Guido Adler.

that even after this reform the harpsichord or the piano found its way into the orchestra as leading instrument. ' The harpsichord ' said Carl Philipp Emmanuel Bach ' is best adapted to maintain a steady time for all the instruments. . . . Its tone is clearly perceptible by all. . . . And if the first violin is placed close by, as it should be, irregularity in performance is easily avoided.' Haydn, when in London, always conducted his symphonies from the harpsichord, while Salomon beat time.*

Without trying to delimit the exact contribution of each individual in the great organic work accomplished simultaneously by several, perhaps many, musicians, it will suffice to say provisionally that at the moment when Haydn began to write his symphonies, the signs considered characteristic of the type were already appearing, singly or collectively, in a considerable number of works from all sources.

The development of his talent in the symphony progresses step by step with the course of his work on the quartet, and cannot be separated from it. Both are elaborations of the sonata form, so beloved by Haydn that an attempt was once made to describe his style in a single phrase, ' Haydn thinks in sonatas '. The plan of composition once accepted, as it quickly was, remains, in fact, identical in its general outlines for all three cases.

Before 1771 he had already written thirty-two quartets and forty-one symphonies, sonatas, trios, *cassations*, or other pieces in similar numbers. His first quartets were called *Quadri* or *Cassations*, though the difference in title indicates no appreciable difference in content. The first twelve are divided into five movements, two

---

* Other more modern examples of the same practice can be quoted. In a performance of *The Creation* at Vienna in 1808, Kreutzer was at the piano, while Salieri conducted. The same parts were played by Umlauf and Wranitzky, respectively, in Beethoven's *The Mount of Olives* at Vienna in 1815.

of which are minuets: the rest have only four movements. The symphonies, like the sonatas, oscillate for
a long time between a division into three movements
and four, the minuet not becoming at once a definite
addition. Of the first twelve symphonies, composed
from 1759 to 1763, which form to-day the first volume
of the complete works, four have no minuet, while one
uses the minuet as finale. Twenty-five years later the
minuet appeared so entirely a mere accessory in the
architecture of a symphony that orchestras felt themselves under no obligation to play those which the
composers included in their works. The autographed
manuscript of the symphony *La Poule*, which Haydn
sent to Paris in 1766, bears the following words in an
unknown hand: ' Minuets to be left out '.*

The idea of the unity of a symphony current at
this period was very far from that which the works of
Beethoven were to establish. It seemed quite natural
to cut up a symphony so as to interpose an air or a
concerto between its first and last movements, or to
play only the allegro or the finale.† The bonds of key
and orchestration united the successive portions by a
very tenuous thread. The principle, optionally admitted
in the old *Suite*, of a theme reappearing several times
under different treatment, had been abandoned. To
return to it again would have been equivalent to a
confession of melodic bankruptcy. The only time that
Haydn tried anything similar, in a sonata, he felt
compelled to explain himself.‡ Anxious, however, to
keep the attention of his hearers on the alert, he care-

---

* That is, the minuet with its trio or *alternativo*.

† See the programmes of the London concerts in Pohl's book, *Haydn
in London*. Habeneck, in 1828, followed this barbarous method when
he divided into two parts the Ninth Symphony of Beethoven.

‡ At the beginning of the collection, he had this notice printed:
' There are two pieces among these six sonatas, in which the same idea
is used in several parts. The composer has done this deliberately, because of the difference in treatment'. See Nohl, *Musiker-Briefe*, p. 83.

fully contrasts the smooth and irregular rhythms of the andante and the allegro, the minuet and the finale.

The plan which he adhered to, and which he continually enlarged and improved, for the first movement, was the fruit of long experiment on the part of his predecessors. They started with a single theme, surrounded only by accessory formulas. Wishing to vary the form of the work, and also to increase its length, they began to use the same motif in two contrasting keys, and then to introduce a second motif, barely outlined at first, but becoming more prominent little by little until it was on an almost equal footing with the first. Becoming bolder, they then reserved a space which grew bigger and bigger, at the beginning of the second section, for a sort of *divertissement* in which the two themes were used for contrapuntal development, until, in conclusion, the first was re-stated in the original key.

All this process is reflected in Haydn's work as in a brilliant mirror. Sandberger, who has written an authoritative study of Haydn's quartets,* finds rudimentary beginnings of thematic development in nine only of the first thirty-two. There is little more in the corresponding symphonies, which owe their charm mainly to the easy, cheerful style which issues from the fertile imagination of youth. The one in E minor, composed in 1772 (No. 44 of the Complete Works, No. 86 in the Wotquenne Catalogue), has been picked out as the first to show any serious design of this kind. That one is an exception, and the symphony, *Les Adieux*, one of the most beautiful and best known of the same period, follows the beaten track. Haydn, however, continues his contrapuntal studies. In 1771, in the 34th, 37th, and 38th quartets, he adds finales, boldly called fugues, with two, three, or four subjects, though we do not know, as Sandberger points out,

---

* Sandberger, *Zur Geschichte des Haydn's Quartetts* in the *Altbayerische Monatsschrift*, Vol. II, Nos. 2 and 3, Munich, 1900.

whether he is voluntarily following the old masters, or intentionally striking out in a new direction. During the ten years from 1771 to 1781, he composed thirty symphonies, but he did not return to the quartet. When this musical form reappears, its evolution is complete, and Haydn rightly describes six quartets of opus 33, dedicated to the Prince von Öttingen-Wallerstein, as compositions in an entirely new style.

It has been said, and must be repeated, that Mozart's influence upon Haydn was decisive at this turning-point of his career.* This influence was reciprocal. Each of the two masters profited by the progress of his friend to enrich his own work with forms and methods invented in brotherly rivalry. At every step forward, they seemed to wait for each other, and to stimulate each other to further progress.

The use of an introduction in slow time, to precede the first allegro and heighten its effect by contrast, was never a fixed rule with Haydn, but he has recourse to it oftener, and with more settled design, in his great symphonies written in London and Paris, than in the earlier ones.

He likes to treat the second movement in variation form; and whether he introduces a series of new themes at each repetition of the subject, or whether he freely embroiders his art with ornament, the ingenuity and fertility of his imagination seem inexhaustible. The same intelligent resourcefulness that the smallest melodic fragment inspires in a skilful master, the same understanding of the proportions to be observed between the nature of a theme and the method of treatment for which it is suitable, enable him in the pretty concluding rondos to reach a point beyond which the

---

* According to the latest research of T. de Wyzewa, it now seems necessary to add that of Clementi, to whom it now appears that Mozart owes the principal elements of this ' entirely new style '. In this connection, see the article by A. Gastoué in the *Courrier Musical* of September-October 1917.

mind of the hearer could not be satisfied, and which could not be passed without destroying the delicate framework of the motifs.

In his quartets, Nos. 39-45, Op. 33 (*Gli Scherzi*), Haydn changed the title of the minuets to *Scherzi*. It is a purely verbal innovation which is justified by no change in the arrangement of the parts. His melodic fancy was at home in this lively, familiar form, which he cultivated for its own sake and by which he set much store. Questioned one day on the precepts laid down by the theorists, and on the attack then being made upon ' consecutive fifths ', he could find no better reply to mock their pedantry than a challenge to write a ' really new minuet '.

In the quartet, though he always bore in mind the skill of his interpreters—he was especially careful in some of the later numbers to show to advantage the talent of Salomon, for whom they were written—Haydn no longer allows the first violin to tyrannize over the other three instruments. Henceforward these latter converse, discuss, or reason with it. Thus, without continuing in the way which his fugal finales had opened, he yet adopts the method of writing in four parts, and by the thematic development and variation fixes the orientation of the modern quartet, which was to gather up the forgotten wealth of the old vocal polyphony.

Strange to say, the master has not the same interest in other forms of chamber music. His sonatas, trios, and various instrumental pieces, often show only a docile compliance with contemporary custom. He was not a clever performer. His first works for the harpsichord were little pieces written for his pupils. Later it was only on rare occasions that he gave a pianist a chance to shine, or even to take much interest in the part he had to play. The other instrumentalists fared little better. His sonatas for piano and violin, like the majority of Mozart's, entrust to the violin only an

I

unimportant part. It plays in unison or accompanies; it is admitted *ad libitum*; it could be taken away without the loss of anything essential from the work.

It is the same, or nearly so, with the wind instruments, oboes and horns, in his first symphonies; but his orchestration does not remain stationary for long. At Esterhaz, having a number of instrumentalists under his orders to play almost nothing but his own works, he experimented at leisure with combinations of tone. His studies in this direction were carried to a considerable length, since we are told that when composing he did not consider merely the general resources of an instrument, but what could be got out of that instrument as played by such and such a performer, who was personally known to him. He has been known to apologize to music lovers who asked him to compose for them, for not being able to suit a sonata to the type of skill of the musician who was to play it, or to the tone of the harpsichord or piano on which it was to be played.* Preoccupation with colour effects thus played a large part in his calculations when composing for orchestra. Yet the historians who have studied his symphonies from this point of view have not been able to point to the introduction of a single unusual instrument, or even to an unusual combination of the usual instruments. Nor have the students of harmony come across any startling finds. Haydn's writing and instrumentation are the essence of clearness, simplicity, and good sense, which leaves no scope for surprise or enthusiasm. Beginning with the string quartet, he ends, in his London symphonies, with the orchestra that satisfied Beethoven up to the *Eroica*—the strings, one or two flutes, two oboes, two horns, two clarinets, one or two bassoons, two trumpets, and a pair of drums. He insists upon an intimate blending of tone. Rarely is an instrument detached from the general effect.

* It will be remembered that Beethoven wrote his Sonata, Op. 106, expressly for the ' Hammerclavier'.

The violin solo in the andante with variations of the eighth London symphony is an exception.

Accustomed to the reign of unbridled virtuosity and to the division of the orchestra into full choir and semi-chorus, the audiences at Salomon's concerts were surprised to see all the instruments participate on their own merits, and answer each other, join and separate, without any one maintaining a constant supremacy over the others. This is the essential characteristic of the symphonic orchestra, which it is one of the greatest achievements of the master of Rohrau to have helped to fix by his admirable compositions.

* * *

Had Haydn any other aim in his instrumental work than the artistic combination of forms and the latent expression of his own mental attitude? Did he intend to give them a literary content, or to conceal a meaning which the audience was invited to discover? There were numerous such examples around him. Johann Kuhnau in 1700 had dedicated his ' musical representations of certain Bible stories in six sonatas ' to the pleasure of all music-lovers. Telemann had written two suites of descriptive pieces for orchestra, one on the mythology of the sea—Thetis sleeping, amorous Neptune, the Tritons, etc.—the other on the adventures of Don Quixote—the fight against the windmills, Rosinante's trot, Sancho derided, etc. When Haydn sent six of his symphonies to Paris, Dittersdorf was writing twelve on Ovid's Metamorphoses, which quickly found warm admirers, eager to praise him for giving his pictures such astonishing exactitude, without changing the established framework. In particular, the minuet, the fixed form of which does not seem to lend itself to strange expressions, in the first symphony, *The Four Ages of the World*, represented ' the despotism which ruled the world during the age of bronze '; in the second symphony, *The Fall of Phaeton*, it expressed the 'transports of Apollo enraged'. In the tenth he left no doubt about Orpheus's promise not to look at Eurydice on coming out of hell. People were amazed at his picture of the peasants changed into frogs, and at a 'suspension' in the violin solo of the eighth symphony—*The Siege of Megara*—which made perceptible to every intelligent listener the leap of a despairing princess, who, throwing herself from the top of a tower, seemed to remain for a moment 'suspended in the air'.*

Such wonderful inventions had no influence on Haydn. His biographers, indeed, tell us that when settling down in the early morning to work on a new symphony, he used to begin by inventing a plot or little story, the events of which he developed and disentangled in his own mind, while covering his ruled paper with notes. These stories, which acted as a slight mental stimulant, must have been extremely simple, for Haydn had neither literary training nor any æsthetic interests apart from music. And we may well believe that he had no more desire to translate into sound a wordless drama or legend than a philosophic abstraction. The 'meanings' that he introduced occasionally into his work have their chief source in the hearty good humour and good sense which form the basis of his character. Gyrowetz found him one day, in London, trying over his 'Surprise' symphony on a little square piano, and rejoicing in the effect that would be produced by the sudden entrance of the kettledrum. 'That will make the ladies jump' he said. On another occasion, when he was setting to music the ten commandments, it amused him to use for the sixth, *Thou shalt not steal*, a theme purloined from Martini. Yet another jest, recorded by Dies, is that of *Jacob's Ladder*, a piece composed in mockery of a violinist who was vain of

* This curious commentary on Dittersdorf's *Metamorphoses of Ovid*, by the pastor Hermes, written in French, was reprinted by Karl Krebs at the end of his little volume entitled *Dittersdorfiana*, Berlin, 1900.

the skill of his left wrist. We might also mention, as a
happy proof of his constant good humour, the little
Children's Symphony, written for string orchestra and
childish instruments, the idea and material of which
were suggested to him by a ' toy fair ' in 1788.

Apart from these fancies, when Haydn, in writing
an instrumental work, leaves the field of pure music
for an excursion into that of descriptive music, he pro-
ceeds by the method of direct imitation of natural
phenomena, the source of inspiration of many parts of
his operas, and almost the whole of his two great oratorios. Imitative motifs explain the titles which he or
his publishers gave to some of the symphonies : *La
Poule*, in which the allegro and andante are discreetly
reminiscent of the cries of the barn-yard; *The Hunt*
and *The Bear*, in which echoes of the hunting field and
heavy rhythms like those of a ' bear dance ' form the
themes of the last movements. The 41st quartet (Op. 33,
No. 3) is sometimes called the ' birds' quartet ', and
the commentators have pointed out, in the first allegro,
the song of the nightingale and the twittering of the
other birds:

21

in the scherzo, which, in this case, precedes the slow
movement, their sleep and their love duets ; in the
adagio their morning hymn ; and in the finale, the
concert of all the birds and the song of the cuckoo. It
is very amusing to see Haydn base a whole movement
on the characteristic third of the cuckoo's song,

22

treated by so many musicians from the Middle Ages
onward, and which he distributes among his four

instruments in responses similar to those which Jannequin used, two and a half centuries before, with such
delightful effect : *

23

Though Haydn never attacked the problem of
psychological expression in his instrumental music,
and failed, even with the help of words, to solve it in
his dramatic music, he remains, none the less, one of
the greatest masters known to history in the realm of
pure music and of musical scene-painting. To what
extent is he able to take possession of our souls, and
by the impress of sheer beauty to inspire in us the mood
of emotional submission to the will of the artist, to
which the commanding or persuasive power of genius

* For the musical text of Jannequin, see Part 7 of *Maîtres musiciens
de la Renaissance Française*, by Henri Expert, or No. 170 of his
Anthologie Chorale.

can give rise in our hearts and minds ? In a word, was
Haydn a poet ? Teodor de Wyzewa denies him this
title, in a page of subtle analysis in which he sets out
to discuss the claims of Giotto and the Siennese painters:
' . . . . I know that it is very difficult to define exactly
what constitutes " poetry " in the plastic arts. Yet it is
undeniable that it does exist there, and that there have
been " poets " and " prose-writers " in painting and
music, just as in literature which is written with words.
Rembrandt and Ruysdael, for instance, are certainly
poets, and the only poets among the Dutch painters,
although they treated the same subjects as Franz Hals
and the Hobbemas.

' Mozart and Joseph Haydn used the same musical
language, in similar conventions. Yet I think no one
could deny that the difference between them lies chiefly
in the fact that Mozart is a " poet ", while Haydn is
not. Similarly in painting, it is now generally agreed
that the old Siennese group were " poets ". They have
this quality to varying extents . . . but all in common
have a certain charm which we feel, without being able
to explain, and which we are irresistibly tempted to
call " poetic ". But though it is difficult, it is not impossible to explain this charm. A poet, in all the arts,
is a man who experiences, on contact with reality,
sensations or emotions finer than the ordinary man's,
and who thus possesses in his soul an instinctive gift,
for making reality more beautiful to us'.*

Haydn, indeed, has not this divine gift. In an art
which has so many branches, it is a sufficient glory for
him to have been an admirable ' prose-writer'. Yet his
prose is by no means always so serious, so earnest, so
calm, or so reasonable, that we cannot recognize in it
a flash of imagination or natural fancy. It is from Heinrich Heine that we shall take a definition of Haydn's
poetic quality, altering the bearing of a passage which

* T. de Wyzewa. *A propos d'une nouvelle biographie de Giotto,* in
the *Revue des Deux Mondes,* 15th September 1905.

the author of the *Reisebilder* wrote about Monsigny. In the music of *The Seasons*, the quartets, and the symphonies, we find ' the serenest grace, an ingenuous sweetness, a freshness like the perfume of the woods, a natural truthfulness . . . and even poetry. No, this last quality is not absent, but it is a poetry without the thrill of the infinite, without the charm of mystery, without bitterness, irony, or morbidity; I might almost say, the poetry of perfect health '.

LIST OF WORKS BY HAYDN

It is impossible to prepare an adequate catalogue of
Haydn's compositions, until the task begun by the
publishers of his *Complete Works* is achieved.

The following list, therefore, is only intended as an
approximate guide to the total production of one of
the most laborious and prolific masters who ever existed.

I Secular Vocal Music

Der Neue Krumme Teufel. Operetta.

*La Marchesa Napola.—La Vedova.—Il Dottore.—Il
Sganarello.* Italian operas performed at Eisenstadt,
1762.

Acide e Galatea. Festa teatrale. Eisenstadt, 1763.

La Canterina. Intermezzo, in two acts. Esterhaz, 1767.

Lo Speziale. Opera buffa, in three acts. *Ibid.*, 1768.

Le Pescatrici. Opera semi-seria, in three acts. *Ibid.*, 1770.

L'Infedelta Delusa. Burletta per musica, in two acts.
Ibid, 1773.

Der Götterrath oder Jupiters Reise auf die Erde. Piece
for marionettes. *Ibid.*, 1773.

Philemon and Baucis. Idem, ibid., 1773.

*Die bestrafte Rachgier oder das abgebrannte Haus. Idem,
ibid.*, 1773.

L'Incontro Improviso. Opera buffa, in three acts. Esterhaz, 1775.

Il Mondo della Luna. Dramma giocoso, in three acts.
Ibid., 1777.

Dido. Piece for marionettes. *Ibid.*, 1777.

Genovefen's vierter Theil. Idem, ibid., 1777.

La Vera Costanza. Dramma giocoso, in three acts. *Ibid.*,
1779.

L'Isola Disabitata. Azione teatrale, in two acts. *Ibid.*,
1779.

La Fedelta Premiata. Dramma giocoso, in two acts.
   Ibid., 1780.
Orlando Paladino. Dramma eroi-comico, in three acts.
   Ibid., 1782.
Armida. Dramma eroico, in three acts. *Ibid.*, 1784.
Orfeo ed Euridice. Opera seria (unfinished). 1791.
Music for the tragedy *Alfred von Cowmeadow.* Vienna,
   1796.
Birthday Cantata for Prince Esterhazy, 1763.
Deutschlands Klage auf den Tod Friedrichs des Grossen.
   Cantata. 1786.
Die Erwählung eines Kapellmeisters. Cantata buffa.
   Vienna.
Dice benissimo. Cantata for one voice and piano. 1782.
Ah, come il cor mi palpita. Idem, 1788.
Arianna a Naxos. Idem, 1790.
Italian cantatas, airs, and duets from various operas
   performed at Esterhaz or in London.
Italian Catch for seven voices. London, 1791.
The Storm. Chorus with orchestra. *Ibid.*, 1792.
Two collections of Twelve Songs, 1782 and 1784.
Thirteen German Songs for three and four voices with
   piano.
Twelve English Ballads, 1792.
The Ten Commandments, in canons, 1794.
Forty-two Canons for several voices.
A Selection of original Scots songs in three parts. In
   three volumes, 1794.
*A Select Collection of original Welsh Airs in three
   parts,* 1794 (forty-one melodies arranged by
   Haydn, the rest by Beethoven and Kozeluch).
Gott erhalte Franz den Kaiser (Austrian Hymn). 1797.

II Religious Music

Missa Brevis, in F, 1750 (No. 11 Novello's edition).
Missa in honorem B.M.V., in E flat, 1766 (No. 12 *idem*).
Missa St. Nicolai, in G, 1772 (No. 7 *idem*).

Missa St. Joannis de Deo, in B flat, 1778 (No. 8 *idem*).
Missa St. Cæcilia, in C, 1780 (No. 5 *idem* and No. 5 Breitkopf and Härtel's edition).
Missa Cellensis, in C, 1780. (No. 15 Novello's edition ; No. 7 Breitkopf and Härtel).
Missa in tempore belli in C (*Paukenmesse*), 1790 (No. 2 in both editions).
Missa Solemnis, in B flat, 1796 (No. 1 *idem*).
Missa Solemnis, in D minor (*Nelson-Messe*), 1798 (No. 3 *idem*).
Missa Solemnis, in B flat (*Theresien-Messe*), 1799 (No. 16 Novello).
Missa Solemnis, in B flat (*Schöpfungsmesse*), 1801 (No. 4 in both editions).
Missa Solemnis, in B flat (*Harmonie-Messe*), 1801 (No. 6 *idem*).

These are the only authentic masses by Haydn. All the others published under his name, notably Nos. 9, 10, 13, and 14 in Novello's edition, are apocryphal.

Stabat Mater with orchestra, 1773, translated into German by Hiller under the title of *The Passion*.

Four *Salve Regina*, two *Ave Regina*, one *Regina Cæli*, two *Te Deum*, and various motets.

Among the large number of motets, offertories, hymns, and fragments of masses, published under Haydn's name, many are arrangements of vocal or instrumental compositions for Latin words. The offertories, *Insanæ et vanæ curæ*, *Audi clamorem*, *Alleluia*, are taken from the oratorio *Il Ritorno di Tobia*.

A *Miserere*, two *Libera*, two *Passions*, and several motets are doubtful or apocryphal. A *Te Deum* in C, attributed to Joseph Haydn, is by his brother Michael. The *Sentences* published under his name are by J. André.

We class with the religious music the *Seven Words of Christ* for orchestra, composed and published in 1785, revised and with vocal parts added for German words in 1801.

III Oratorios

Il Ritorno di Tobia, 1775. Revised in 1784.
Die Schöpfung, 1798.
Die Jahreszeiten, 1801.
Fragments of an English oratorio, on a translation of
a poem by Seldon, *Mare Clausum*, 1794.
The oratorio *Abramo ed Isacco*, assigned to Haydn, is
by Misliweczek.

IV Instrumental Music

The classification and enumeration of Haydn's instrumental works into the various types can only be
attempted at present incompletely and provisionally.

According to the statements of the early biographers,
the number of symphonies was long fixed at 118.
Subsequently increased to 144 (Leopold Schmidt), 149
(Wotquenne), 153 (Hadow), it is now definitely reduced to 104 by the publishers of the Complete Works,
who have placed a chronological and thematic list of
Haydn's symphonies at the beginning of their first
volume. In addition to the 104 authentic symphonies,
this list includes thirty-eight apocryphal symphonies
now restored to their true authors (Michael Haydn,
Leopold Hoffman, Dittersdorf, Vanhal, etc.), thirty-
six which are still doubtful, and twelve *overtures* which
are actually Haydn's and which were formerly classed
as symphonies.

Related to the symphonies is the long series of *cassations, divertissements, serenades*, and *nocturnes*, for
orchestra or small groups of instruments.

Haydn did not disdain to write collections of *minuets*
and *danses allemandes* for orchestra, containing alto-
gether nearly eighty pieces, for balls in London and
Vienna.

His *concertos, concertinos, symphonies concertantes*, and
divertissements, for one or several instruments (violin,

violoncello, baryton, lira, piano, flute, or horn), with
accompaniment by orchestra or by quartet, number
about 50.

Haydn's collected string quartets number eighty-
three, reduced to seventy-seven when we take away the
arrangement as quartet of the *Seven Words of Christ*
which the publishers usually include.

There are about thirty trios for strings, thirty-eight
piano trios, fifteen trios for wind and strings combined,
four sonatas for piano and violin, fifty-two sonatas,
divertissements, and other pieces for piano alone.

The pieces for the baryton, alone or accompanied,
and for the lira, number about two hundred.

It is often difficult to discover the original form of
works which have been arranged and published in
different versions.

To mention only the most famous example, there
are no less than one hundred and twenty editions of
the Austrian Hymn as a separate composition, exclud-
ing the arrangement of the string quartet in which it is
often inserted with variation. The *Minuet du Boeuf,*
rendered popular by an entirely imaginary story, has
been printed no less frequently. It is easy to understand
the confusion found in the catalogues when the com-
pilers have to mention, according to their arrangement,
under many different heads, pieces having no other
description than indications of time and key.

BIBLIOGRAPHY

ADAM, Adolphe. *Derniers Souvenirs d'un Musicien.* Lévy, Paris, 1859. pp. 1-38, the youth of Haydn.

ADLER, Guido. Preface to Vol. XV, part ii, of *Denkmäler der Tonkunst in Österreich* (symphonies of the Viennese school). Artaria, Vienna, 1908.

—— *Festrede zur Haydn-Zentenarfeier in Wien.* Artaria, Vienna, 1909.

Allgemeine Deutsche Biographie, Vol. XI. Leipzig, 1880, pp. 123-148, article *Haydn (Franz-Joseph),* by R. von Liliencron and W. H. Riehl; pp. 148-157, article *Haydn (Johann-Michael)* by Schafhautl.

ARNOLD, Ign. F. *Joseph Haydn, Seine kurze Biographie und ästetische Darstellung seiner Werke.* Erfurt, 1810. Pp. 272. 2nd edition 1825; reproduced in the author's book, *Gallerie der berühmtesten Tonkünstler.*

BARBEDETTE, H. *Haydn, sa vie et ses œuvres.* In the *Ménestrel,* year 1870-1871.

BECKER, Carl Ferd. *Joseph Haydn.* Leipzig, 1832 (*Die Zeitgenossen* Series). *Biographische Skizze von Michael Haydn. Von den verklärten Tonkünstlers Freunden entworfen, und zum Besten seiner Wittwe herausgegeben.* Salzburg, 1808 (by Otter and Schimm).

BITTER, C. H. *Eine Studie zum 'Stabat Mater'.* Leipzig, 1833 (pp. 57 ff., Haydn's *Stabat*).

BOMBET, H. Beyle. *Lettres écrites de Vienne en Autriche sur le célèbre compositeur Joseph Haydn suivies d'une Vie de Mozart . . .* Didot, Paris, 1814, pp. 468 (Fraudulent translation of *Haydine* by Carpani). Reprinted as *Vies de Haydn, de Mozart, et de Métastase* under the name of Stendhal, Paris, 1817. Several editions, Lévy, Paris. English translation, London, 1817.

Bouillat. *J. Haydn.* Bloud, Paris, 1901 (*Les Contemporains* Series).

Brendel. *Geschichte der Musik in Italien, Deutschland, und Frankreich.* Leipzig, 1852. 6th edition, 1878, pp. 274-280.

Brenet, Michel. *Histoire de la Symphonie à orchestre depuis ses origines jusqu'à Beethoven.* Gauthier-Villars, Paris, 1882.

—— *Les Concerts en France sous l'ancien régime.* Fischbacher, Paris, 1900.

Carpani, Giuseppe. *Le Haydine, ovvero lettere sulla vita e sulle opere del celebre maestro Giuseppe Haydn.* Milan, 1812. 2nd edition, Padua, 1823. Pp. xii + 306. Plagiarised version by Henri Beyle, see above under Bombet. French translation, *Haydn, sa Vie, ses Ouvrages, ses Voyages, et ses Aventures,* translated by D. Mondo, Paris, 1837, pp. 367.

Conrat, H. *Joseph Haydn und der Croatische Volksgesang.* In *Die Musik,* 4th year, 1904-5, vol. vii, pp. 14-29.

Cramer, Karl Friedrich. *Über die Schönheiten und den Ausdruck der Leidenschaft in einer Cantate von J. Haydn.* In the *Magazin der Musik,* Vol. I, 1783, pp. 1073-1115.

Deldevez. *Curiosités Musicales.* Didot, Paris, 1873, pp. 3-53.

Dies, Albert Chr. *Biographische Nachrichten von Joseph Haydn, nach mündlichen Erzählungen derselben entworfen und herausgegeben von . . .* Vienna, 1810, pp. x + 220.

Döring, H. *Biographie und Characteristik von Joseph Haydn.* Wolfenbüttel, undated.

Duesberg, J. *Visite d'Iffland à Haydn* (from a German paper). In the *Revue et Gazette musicale,* 14th November 1858.

Eberwein, J. *Vater Haydn, ein dramatisches Gedicht.* Matthes, Leipzig, 1863, pp. vii + 47.

EITNER, Robert. *Biographisches und bibliographisches Quellen-Lexikon der Musiker* . . . Vol. V, Leipzig, 1901, pp. 59-76.

ERSCH and GRUBER. *Allgemeine Encyclopädie der Wissenschaften und Künste*, 1828, Section II, Vol. III, pp. 239-256, article *Jos. Haydn*, and pp. 256-259, article *Michael Haydn*, by Fröhlich.

Essai historique sur la vie de Joseph Haydn. Strassburg, 1812.

FÉTIS. *Biographie universelle des musiciens*. 2nd edition, Vol. IV, pp. 254-271.

FRAMERY. *Notice sur Joseph Haydn, contenant quelques particularités de sa vie privée, relatives à sa personne et à ses ouvrages*. Paris, 1810.

GAMBARA. *Haydn coronato in Elicona*, poemetto. Brescia, 1819, pp. 30.

GERHARD, C. *Der Humor in der Musik*. In *Die Gegenwart*, 15th November 1902.

GHISI. *Elogio Storico di Giuseppe Haydn*. Florence, 1839, pp. 16.

GRIESINGER, G. A. *Biographische Notizen über Joseph Haydn*. Leipzig, 1810, pp. 126.

GROSSER. *Biographische Notizen über Joseph Haydn nebst einer kleinen Sammlung interessanter Anecdoten und Erzählungen*. Hirschberg, 1826, pp. xviii + 107.

GROVE, Sir George. *Dictionary of Music and Musicians*. 2nd edition by Fuller-Maitland, Vol. I, p. 633, article *Creation*; p. 779, article *Emperor's Hymn*. Vol. II (1906), pp. 348-370, article *Haydn*, by C. F. Pohl, with additions by W. H. Hadow. Vol. III (1907), pp. 474-510, article *Oratorio*, by Rockstro and E. Walker. Vol. IV, pp. 504-535, article *Sonata*, by C. H. Parry, and pp. 763-797, article *Symphony* by the same.

HADDEN, J. Cuthbert. *George Thomson* . . . *His Life and Correspondence* (with Haydn and Beethoven). London, 1898.

K

—— *Haydn*. Dent, London, 1902, pp. 244.

HADOW, Sir W. H. *A Croatian Composer: Notes towards the Study of Joseph Haydn*. Seeley, London, 1897.

—— *The Oxford History of Music*. Vol. V, The Viennese Period. Clarendon Press, Oxford, 1904.

HANSLICK, Ed. *Geschichte des Concertwesens in Wien*. Braumüller, Vienna, 1869.

HASE, H. von. *Joseph Haydn und Breitkopf und Härtel*. Leipzig, 1909.

HAWEIS, Rev. H. R. *Music and Morals*. Daildy, London, 1879, pp. 241-263.

HENRICI, Dr. *Die Schöpfung, von Haydn*. Goslar, 1828.

HETSCH, G. *Joseph Haydn*. Copenhagen, 1901, pp. 80. (In Danish).

HOCKER, G. *Das grosse Dreigestirn—Haydn, Mozart, Beethoven—in biographischen Erzählungen*. Flemming, Glogau, 1898.

HUMPERDINCK, E. *Joseph Haydns Symphonie in Es dur, erläutert*. (*Der Musikführer*, No. 6). Bechhold, Frankfurt-am-Main, 1894, pp. 16.

Iffland bei Haydn (In *Bühne und Welt*, year 1901, No. 19).

Joseph Haydn, seine Biographie. (*Neujahrsstücke der allgemeinen Musikgesellschaft in Zürich*, Nos. 18 and 19). Zürich, 1830-1831, pp. 28.

Joseph Haydns handschriftliches Tagebuch aus der Zeit seines zweiten Aufenthaltes in London, 1794 und 1795. Breitkopf und Härtel, Leipzig, 1909.

KARAJAN, Th. von. *Haydn in London, 1791-2*. Gerold, Vienna, 1861, pp. 118.

KINKER. *Ter Nachgedachtenis van Joseph Haydn*. Amsterdam, 1810.

KREBS, Karl. *Haydn, Mozart, Beethoven*. (*Aus Natur- und Geisteswelt*, Vol. XCII). Teubner, Leipzig and Berlin, 1906, pp. 4-41.

KRETZSCHMAR, H. *Führer durch den Concertsaal*. Vol. I, 3rd edition. Breitkopf and Härtel, Leipzig, 1898, pp. 51-108 (symphonies). Vol. II, 2nd edition, *ibid.*, 1895, pp. 118-123, 163-164, 185, 281, etc. (religious works). Vol. II, pt. II, 2nd edition, 1899, pp. 221-244 (oratorios).

KRUTSCHEK, Paul. *Der Messentypus von Haydn bis Schubert.* In the *Kirchenmusikalisches Jahrbuch für das Jahr* 1893, pp. 109-119.

KUHAC, Fr. S. *Josip Haydn i Hrvatske narodne popievke.* Zagreb, 1881.

—— *Chansons nationales des Slaves du Sud.* Zagreb (Agram), 1879-1884, 3 vols.

LA FAGE, J. A. de. *Notice sur la vie et les ouvrages de Haydn.* In the *Annales de la Société libre des Beaux-Arts,* year 1840-1, pp. 67-113. Reproduced in the same author's book, *Miscellanées musicales,* Paris, 1844.

LAJARTE, Th. de. *Histoire d'un oratorio et d'une machine infernale.* In the *Nouvelle Revue,* 1st January 1885.

LAVOIX, Henri. *Histoire de l'instrumentation.* Didot, Paris, 1878, pp. 281-294.

LE BRETON, Joachim. *Notice historique sur la vie et les ouvrages de Haydn, membre associé de l'Institut de France et d'un grand nombre d'Académies.* Paper read at a public meeting of a group of the *Académie des Beaux-Arts,* 6th October 1810. Paris, 1810.

LORENZ, Dr. Franz. *Haydn, Mozart, und Beethoven's Kirchenmusik.* Leuckart, Breslau, 1866, pp. viii + 96.

LUDWIG, C. A. *Joseph Haydn, ein Lebensbild.* Buchting, Nordhausen, 1867, pp. 213.

MASON, D. G. *Beethoven and his Forerunners.* Macmillan, London, 1904, pp. 173-209.

MAYR, G. S. *Breve notizie istoriche della vita e delle opere di Giuseppe Haydn.* Bergamo, 1809, pp. 14.

MICHEL, Henri. *La Sonate pour clavier avant Beethoven.* Fischbacher, Paris, 1908, pp. 75-97.

Musikalische Briefe, Wahrheit über Tonkunst und Tonkünstler, von einem Wohlbekannten (J. C. Lobe). Baumgartner, Leipzig, 1860, pp. 172-180.

NAEGELI, Hans Georg. *Vorlesungen über Musik mit Berücksichtigung der Dilettanten.* Cotta, Stuttgart, 1826.

NEF, KARL. *Vergessene Gesänge von J. Haydn.* In the *Schweizerische Musikzeitung,* 40th year, 1901, No. 36.

NEUKOMM, E. *Dix-huit mois de la vie de Haydn.* In the *Revue et Gazette musicale de Paris,* year 1874, several articles.

—— *Michel Haydn.* In the *Chronique musicale,* 1st year, 1873, Vol. II, pp. 282-288, and 2nd year, 1874, Vol. III, pp. 119-124 and 161-165.

NIGGLI, A. *Joseph Haydn, Sein Leben und Wirken: Vortrag.* Schweighauser, Basel, 1882.

NOHL, Ludwig. *Musiker-Briefe.* Duncker, Leipzig, 1867, pp. 73-174.

—— *Haydn, Eine Biographie.* Reclam, Leipzig, undated.

PARENT, H. *Répertoire encyclopédique du pianiste.* Hachette, Paris. Vol. I, 1900, pp. 46-54.

PAZDIREK, Fr. *Manuel universel de la littérature musicale, guide pratique et complet de toutes les éditions,* etc. Costallat, Paris, and Pazdirek, Vienna. Vol. XI, 1907, pp. 238-271.

PERGER. Preface to Vol. XIV, Part II, of the *Denkmäler der Tonkunst in Österreich.* (Instrumental music of Michael Haydn.)

POHL, Carl Ferdinand. *Joseph Haydn.* Vol. I. Breitkopf and Härtel, Leipzig, 1878, pp. xviii + 423, 1 plate and 1 portrait. Vol. II, *idem,* 1882, pp. viii + 383 + 14, 1 portrait.

—— *Mozart und Haydn in London.* Zweite Abtheilung, *Haydn in London.* Gerold, Vienna, 1867, pp. xvi + 390.

REIMANN, H. *Musikalische Rückblicke.* Berlin, 1900. Vol. I, pp. 79-87. *Haydn's und Beethoven's angebliche Plagiate aus Kroatischen Volksliedern.*

REINECKE, Karl. *Meister der Tonkunst: Mozart, Beethoven, Haydn, Weber, Schumann, Mendelssohn.* Spemann, Stuttgart, 1902, pp. 249-316.

REISSMANN, August. *Joseph Haydn, sein Leben und seine Werke.* Gutentag, Berlin, 1880, pp. 263 + 43 (music), 1 portrait.

RIEHL, W. H. *Musikalische Charakterköpfe.* 2nd edition. Cotta, Stuttgart, Vol. III, pp. 302-339.

RIEMANN, Hugo. Preface to the Symphonies of the Mannheim School before the volume, *Denkmäler deutscher Tonkunst, Zweite Folge, Denkmäler der Tonkunst in Bayern.* Dritter Jahrgang. Vol. I, Breitkopf and Härtel, Leipzig, 1902.

RITTER, Hermann. *Haydn, Mozart, Beethoven.* Bamberg, 1897, pp. 17-26.

SANDBERGER, Adolf. *Zur Geschichte des Haydn's Quartetts.* In the *Altbayerische Monatsschrift,* Vol. II, Nos. 2 and 3. Stahl, Munich, 1900.

—— *Zur Entstehungsgeschichte von Haydn's SIEBEN WORTE DES ERLÖSERS AM KREUZE.* In the *Jahrbuch der Musikbibliothek Peters* for 1903, pp. 47-59.

SAUZAY, Eug. *Haydn, Mozart, Beethoven. Étude sur le quatuor.* Didot, Paris, 1861, pp. 37-72.

SCHIEDERMAYER, L. *Die Blütezeit der Öttingen-Wallerstein'schen Hofkapelle.* In the *Recueil trimestriel de la Société Internationale de Musique,* 9th year, 1907-8, 1st number (pp. 105-106, Haydn).

SCHILLING, G. *Encyclopädie der gesammten musikalischen Wissenschaften.* Vol. III, Stuttgart, 1836, pp. 518-526, article *Haydn,* by Ad. B. Marx.

SCHMID, Anton. *Joseph Haydn und Nicolo Zingarelli: Beweisführung, dass Joseph Haydn der Tonsetzer des allgemein beliebten österreichischen Volks- und Festgesanges sei.* Holzel, Vienna, 1847, pp. 121.

SCHMID, Otto. *Johann Michael Haydn.* In *Die Musik,* 5th year, 1905-6, No. 21, pp. 159-163.

—— *Johann Michael Haydn: Sein Leben und Wirken.* (*Musikalisches Magazin,* No. 16). Beyer, Langensalza, 1906, pp. 19.

SCHMIDT, Leopold. *Joseph Haydn.* (*Berühmte Musiker*

Series.) Harmonie Gesellschaft, Berlin, 1898, pp. 136, illustrated.

SCHNYDER VON WARTENSEE. *Aesthetische Betrachtungen über die Jahreszeiten von Joseph Haydn.* Keller, Frankfurt-am-Main, 1861. 2nd edition, pp. 15.

SEEBURG, Franz von. *Joseph Haydn, eine Biographie.* (Written for the young: several editions in French, German, and English.)

SHEDLOCK, J. S. *The Pianoforte Sonata, its Origin and Development.* Methuen, London, 1895, pp. 111-120.

SIEBIGK, C. A. *Museum berühmter Tonkünstler in Kupfern und schriftlichen Abrissen.* Breslau, 1881. (Haydn, 32 pages and portrait.)

S. I. M. No. 1 of the 6th year (1910), *Hommage à Haydn*, articles and unpublished illustrations, by T. de Wyzewa, L. Greilsamer, W. Ritter, Tandler, G. Lyon.

STENDHAL. See BOMBET and CARPANI.

TAPPERT, W. *Die Österreichische Nationalhymne.* In *Die Musik*, 4th year, 1904-5, No. 18, pp. 415-416.

TEIBLER. *Joseph Haydn's Symphonie in G-dur* (Military). . . . *Idem in C-dur* (The South) . . . *Idem in C-dur* (The Bear). (*Der Musikführer*, Nos. 184, 215, 234, Schlesinger, Berlin).

TOWNSEND, P. D. *Joseph Haydn.* (*Great Musicians* Series). Sampson, London, 1884, pp. 130.

Über die angeblich von J. Haydn componirten 'Spruchwörter'. In the *Allgemeine Musikalische Zeitung*, Leipzig, New Series, 5th year, Nos. dated 9th March and 27th April 1870. (By L. von Stetter and Chrysander.)

Über Joseph Haydn's Streichquartette, insbesondere im Arrangement für das Clavier zu vier Händen. In the *Allegmeine Musikalische Zeitung*, Leipzig, New Series, 6th year, Nos. dated 8th and 15th February 1871. (By L. von Steller.)

Viotta, H. *De Verdiensten van Haydn ten opzicht der Toonkunst.* In *De Gids*, June 1901.

Vogel, Emil. *Joseph Haydn's Portraits.* In the *Jahrbuch der Musikbibliothek Peters*, 5th year, 1908, pp. 13-26.

Wendschuh, L. *Über Jos. Haydn's Opern. Dissertation.* Kammerer, Halle, 1897, pp. 145 + 3.

Widman, B. *Jos. Haydn's Schöpfung.* (*Der Musikführer*, Nos. 13, 14). Bechhold, Frankfurt-am-Main, 1894.

—— *Jos. Haydn's Die Jahreszeiten.* (*Idem*, Nos. 8 and 85.) *Ibid.*

—— *Jos. Haydn's Symphonie in G-dur* (Oxford). . . . *Symphonie in G-dur* (mit dem Paukenschlag). (*Idem*, Nos. 50 and 59). *Ibid.*

Wotquenne, Alfred. *Catalogue de la bibliothèque du Conservatoire royal de Bruxelles.* Vol. II. Coosemans, Brussels, 1902, pp. 464-485, with 7 pages of music. (Catalogue of Haydn's symphonies.)

Wurzbach von Tannenberg. *Joseph Haydn und sein Bruder Michael: Zwei bio-bibliographischen Künstler-Skizzen.* Lechner, Vienna, 1862, pp. 48.

Zohrer, F. *Der Fürst der Musik, eine Erzählung aus dem Leben Haydn's.* (*Österreichiche Jugendbücher.*) Teschen, 1906.

The celebrations of the centenary of Haydn's death, in May 1909, prompted the publication in reviews and literary or musical periodicals of a multitude of articles, most of which will be found catalogued in numbers of the *Bulletin Mensuel de la Société internationale de Musique*, years 1909 and 1910.

INDEX

137

INDEX

INDEX

INDEX

INDEX

INDEX 143

INDEX

INDEX

INDEX

INDEX

INDEX

INDEX